Land's End Circuit

Max Landsberg

Rucksack Readers

Land's End Circuit

Published 2020, by Rucksack Readers,
6 Old Church Lane, Edinburgh, EH15 3PX, UK
tel   +44/0 131 661 0262
email   info@rucsacs.com
web   *www.rucsacs.com*

© text Max Landsberg; photographs © licensors as listed on page 71.

The right of Max Landsberg to be identified as the author of this work has been asserted by him in accordance with the Copyright, Designs and Patents Act 1988.

All rights reserved. No part of this publication may be reproduced, stored in a retrieval system, or transmitted in any form or by any means, electronic, mechanical, photocopying, recording or otherwise, without prior permission in writing from the publisher and copyright holders.

ISBN 978-1-898481-92-8

British Library cataloguing in publication data: a catalogue record for this book is available from the British Library.

Designed in Scotland by Ian Clydesdale (*www.workhorse.scot*)

Printed and bound by Blackmore, UK on rainproof, biodegradable paper

Mapping is © Rucksack Readers and was created specially for this book by Lovell Johns. It contains Ordnance Survey data © Crown copyright and database rights 2020 with further material collected by the author.

Publisher's note

All information was checked prior to publication. However, changes are inevitable: take local advice and look out for signage e.g. for temporary diversions. Walkers should check two websites for updates before setting out: *www.rucsacs.com/books/lec* and *bit.ly/SWCP-route.*

The weather in Cornwall is unpredictable, especially on the coastal cliffs, and some parts of the route are exposed and remote. Do not rely on having mobile phone reception. You are responsible for your own safety, and for ensuring that your clothing, food and equipment are suited to your needs. The publisher cannot accept any liability for any ill-health, accident or loss arising directly or indirectly from reading this book.

Feedback is welcome and will be rewarded

We appreciate comments and suggestions, and many improvements in this edition reflect reader feedback. Feedback is always welcome, and if your input leads us to make changes, you will be entitled to claim a free book. Please email us at *info@rucsacs.com*.

Contents

Introduction	4
1 Planning and preparation	5
Getting there and away	6
Time of year and weather	7
Duration and stages	8
Accommodation and facilities	8
Gradients and terrain	10
Waymarking and navigation	11
Buses in western Cornwall	12
Countryside Code and safety	13
Packing checklist	14
Cornish language, placenames and pronunciation	15
2 Background information	
2·1 Landscape and its formation	16
2·2 History of Cornwall	19
2·3 Mining	21
2·4 Habitats and wildlife	23
3 The route in detail	
St Ives	28
3·1 St Ives to Zennor Head	30
3·2 Zennor Head to the Crowns	36
3·3 The Crowns to Land's End	41
3·4 Land's End to Lamorna	46
3·5 Lamorna to Penzance	54
Penzance	58
Beyond Penzance	59
St Michael's Mount	60
4 St Ives via St Michael's Way	62
5 Reference	
Development, visitor info and support services	70
Further reading	70
Maps, GPS, transport and travel, and weather	71
Acknowledgements and credits	71
Index	72

Introduction

Where Cornwall's rolling heathland juts abruptly into the wild Atlantic Ocean, this circuit of Land's End offers a week's walking around some of England's most spectacular and intriguing coastline.

It also serves as an introduction to the South West Coast Path (SWCP). For walkers tempted by that 630-mile (1014-km) challenge, it makes sense to taste the experience before committing yourself to completion. For most people, the SWCP requires about 45-60 walking days. Our section amounts to less than a tenth of its total length, but provides its scenic appeal in abundance.

From St Ives to Penzance, our circuit follows the SWCP step for step – along high cliff-tops, through smugglers coves and fishing villages, past 19th century mines that are now World Heritage Sites, beside prehistoric remains, and down narrow crooked lanes that once hid pirates and are now home to art galleries.

Eventually you arrive at numinous Saint Michael's Mount, perhaps in the company of dolphins or otters, and with a perfect sunset if you are lucky. The geology of this last promontory to be added to England is exposed and inviting. To complete our circuit, follow the pilgrimage route of Saint Michael's Way past its holy wells and churches, northward to St Ives.

While Land's End might appear distant from where you live, this route is brought nearer by its remarkably convenient access. Both St Ives and Penzance are served with regular public transport from London and elsewhere, so you can start at either point and proceed anticlockwise (as we recommend) or clockwise.

Welcome to the myth, mines, light and culture of Cornwall … or as said in the Cornish language: *dynnargh dhis*!

South-west from Land's End

Planning and preparation

This route consists of a coastal section of 42 miles (67 km) following the waymarked SWCP National Trail around the Penwith peninsula between St Ives and Penzance. From Penzance you can head east to Marazion to visit the famous St Michael's Mount: see pages 60-61. Afterwards, either return home or complete the circuit with a return walk of about 9 miles (14 km) along the pilgrimage route of St Michael's Way: see pages 62-69.

We describe the route anticlockwise from St Ives to Penzance. Most guidebooks and other resources for the SWCP are organised in the anticlockwise direction: by tradition the full SWCP starts from Minehead, Somerset and ends at Poole in Dorset.

A possible reason to walk in the reverse direction is if you expect the wind to blow from east to west on the days that you walk: first check the weather forecast. For longer-term planning, be aware of how variable the wind direction can be: see page 7 for a typical wind rose. Predictions of wind and weather can be unreliable, especially at longer range.

If you intend to complete the full circuit anticlockwise, you could start from Penzance instead of St Ives, and complete St Michael's Way northbound before walking the coastal section. Both towns are well-served by public transport.

Finally, you can walk St Michael's Way in either direction, using a convenient bus to take you from one end of the Way to the other. Walking southbound lets you follow in the footsteps of the departing pilgrims of long ago. Further options are explained on pages 59 and 69.

Most of the route is a public footpath, not a bridleway or cycle route, so cycling is not normally allowed except between Mousehole and Marazion.

Good bus services run along and around the peninsula, offering flexibility to include both fitter and less fit members in the same walking group. They also offer useful escape options if your itinerary turns out to have been over-ambitious: see page 12.

Getting there and away

For most people, the easiest access to the route is by train, especially if coming via London.

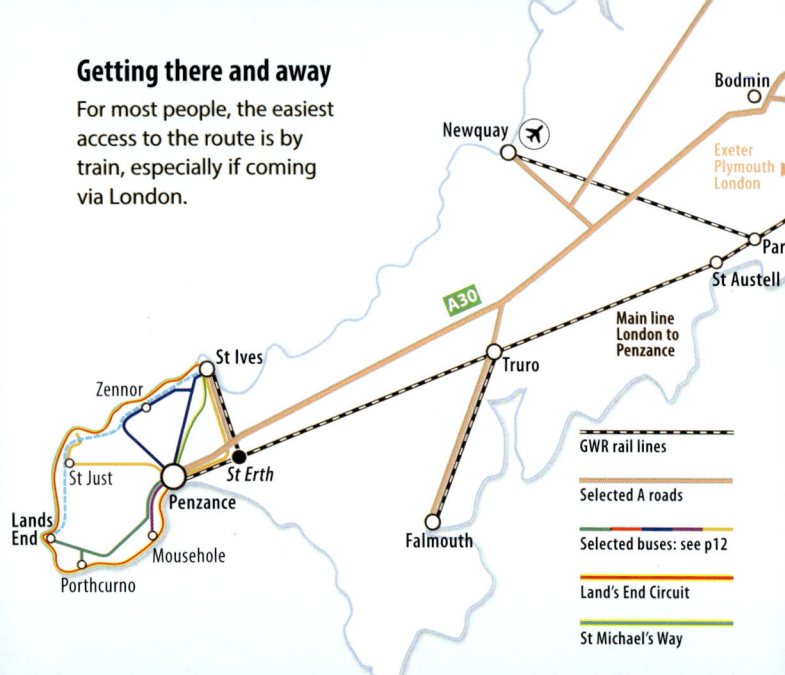

On a typical weekday there are 17 trains from London Paddington to Penzance, with an average journey time of 5 hours 50 minutes, and also the Riviera Sleeper that takes 8 hours overnight. From Paddington to St Ives there are 33 trains daily, journey time 7 hours 40 minutes on average. There are also good connections northwards via Bristol and Gloucester.

Penzance and St Ives can also be accessed by good bus connections: check the schedules of National Express and Megabus. For those that choose to arrive by car, St Ives and Penzance have long-stay car parks.

Distances and approximate journey times between selected places

	miles	km	by train	by bus	by car
London – Penzance	283	460	5h 30m	9h 15m	6h 00m
Bristol – Penzance	190	306	4h 15m	7h 15m	4h 00m
London – Land's End	294	475			7h 15m
Bristol – Land's End	195	310			4h 30m

Time of year and weather

According to climate statistics, the circuit is best walked between mid-June and mid-September. At other times of year you may experience more solitude and, if you can decide to depart at short notice (within 2 weeks), there is a case for going on a good weather forecast – provided that you can still find accommodation. In season, aim to avoid holiday weekends and festivals when St Ives and Penzance can become crowded. Check online for dates.

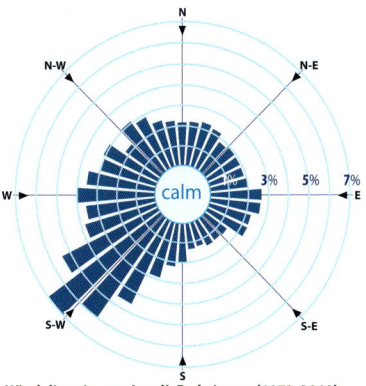

Wind directions at Land's End airport (1973-2019)
Length of bar shows proportion of winds blowing from that direction; data from Iowa State University, see page 71

The coastal section of this route is exposed not only to the elements, but also to Atlantic weather systems. Wear clothing and footwear that will deal with unpredictable rain, blustery wind, and occasional bogginess. Take account of the additional effort of walking into the wind. Walking into a 30 mph wind can be difficult, at 40 mph you could be blown off balance and at 60 mph safe progress is almost impossible.

Always check for a recent weather forecast before setting out: see page 71. Bear in mind that wind speed forecasts are typically for sea level. Wind speeds increase with height, and over a cliff-top could be double the speed at sea level. Fasten your hat, and avoid exposed cliff edges and ledges.

Finally, ensure you can navigate even if suddenly immersed in mist or fog. See page 11 for waymarking and navigation.

Storm lashes Longships Lighthouse, off Land's End

Duration and stages

The number of days needed to complete the coastal section will depend on your level of fitness. It will also depend crucially on how long you take to view or visit the many sites along the way. For walkers in a hurry, we show a four-day option in the table opposite. In theory the walk could be compressed into three days by overnighting at Zennor and Sennen Cove only, but that would involve two very long, tough days of 16 and 18 miles (26 and 29 km) respectively and we do not recommend it.

That said, most walkers can complete the coastal route enjoyably in five days, corresponding to the five chapters of Part 3. There are further options to break the route into shorter stages that may help you accommodate different times of arrival and departure. They are shown in Table 2 on page 9. Remember that accommodation may be very limited.

St Michael's Way can easily be completed with just one further walking day. When planning your dates, note that St Michael's Mount castle and gardens are closed on Saturdays and on other days during the winter; causeway and ferry details are given at www.stmichaelsmount.co.uk/plan-your-visit.

Table 1: split the walk over four or five days

	mi	km	mi	km
St Ives				
	7·2	11·6	7·2	11·6
Zennor Head				
			9·1	14·7
The Crowns	11·3	18·2		
Cape Cornwall			8·7	13·9
Land's End	11·5	18·5		
Porthcurno			10·4	16·7
Lamorna	11·5	18·5		
			6·1	9·8
Penzance				
Total (rounded)	42	67	42	67

Accommodation and facilities

Your options for accommodation include various hotels and B&Bs (typically some distance off-route), two hostels, and a fair supply of camping sites. The table opposite indicates the main facilities available on or near the route as of January 2020. The SWCP National Trail Companion booklet and website offer further listings and are updated frequently.

Although many locations offer accommodation, most are small villages, often with very few beds available. So book early – especially in the popular summer months. If places close to the route are fully booked, do not give up: more distant lodgings may be feasible. Find out if your B&B host will collect and drop off if arranged in advance, or consider using a taxi. In 2020, a taxi or Uber fare of about £8 could extend your range by up to 10 miles/ 16 km. There are bus stops in all the places listed in the table with the exceptions of Porthmeor Cove and Porthgwarra.

Note that you can have your baggage transported by a commercial company – see page 70. Some provide a full service including booking your accommodation.

With careful pacing, you might manage to pitch your tent at commercial campsites using the National Trail's online resources for updated details: see page 70. You are not allowed to 'wild camp' unless you have obtained permission from the relevant landowner before pitching your tent.

The Dolphin Tavern, Penzance

Cornwall is blessed with many cafés, ice cream shops and pubs, and in most sections walkers will easily find refreshments without having to go more than 1 km or so offroute. However, remember that having plenty of drinking water is vital to your wellbeing, especially in warm weather.

Table 2: facilities along the route

	miles	km	Distance offroute (km)	B&B / hotel	hostel	pub/ café	shop (food)
St Ives (station)				✓	✓	✓	✓
Zennor Head	7·2	11·	Zennor 0·8	✓	✓	✓	
Gurnard's Head	2·1	3·4	Treen 0·4			✓	
Porthmeor Cove	1·0	1·6				✓	
Pendeen Lighthouse	3·9	6·3	Pendeen 0·5	✓		✓	✓
The Crowns	2·1	3·4	Botallack 1·0	✓		✓	
Cape Cornwall	2·0	3·2	St Just 2·0	✓	✓	✓	✓
Sennen Cove	5·5	8·9		✓		✓	✓
Land's End	1·1	1·8	Trevescan 1·3	✓		✓	
Porthgwarra	3·5	5·7		◆		✓	
Porthcurno	1·3	2·1	Trethewey 1·3, Treen 1·3	◆		✓	
Lamorna	5·5	8·9	Bus-stop 1·5	◆		✓	
Mousehole	2·4	3·9		✓		✓	✓
Newlyn	1·9	3·1		✓		✓	✓
Penzance (station)	1·7	2·8		✓	✓	✓	✓
Marazion (Chapel Rock)	3·0	4·9		✓		✓	✓
Ludgvan	1·6	2·5				✓	
St Ives (station)	7·3	11·8		✓	✓	✓	✓
				◆ various B&Bs inland			

Gradients and terrain

The route undulates significantly. Many walkers are taken aback that a relatively short distance on the map can be so tiring, that they sweat so much and drink so much, and that the final stretch to the night's lodging requires a hill climb. The total ascent (including all the ups and downs) for the route is nearly 3000 metres (9840 ft), mostly concentrated within four days. Although the highest point of the coastal section is a mere 118 m (387 ft) above sea level, the 50-metre contour is crossed more than 40 times. From this point of view, the route definitely qualifies as 'hillwalking' and if you normally use walking poles on hilly gradients, you will be glad of them here.

The circuit primarily follows public footpaths, though there are short sections of road within St Ives and between Mousehole and Penzance and Marazion, as well as along St Michael's Way. The route tends to be hard and gravelly underfoot, since it is traversing granite. Some sections can be boggy after rain though these areas are relatively few and short. In a few places you might use your hands to steady yourself when negotiating an incline, but this is definitely a walking route, not a scramble.

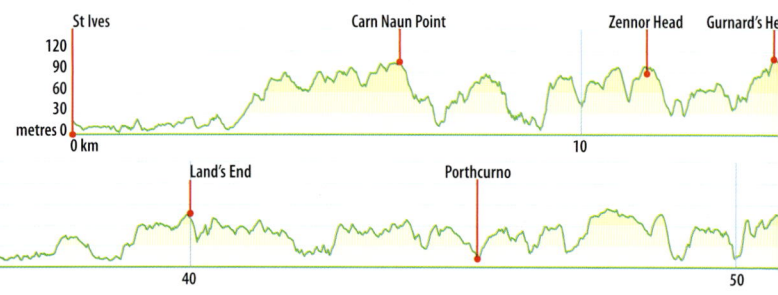

Waymarking and navigation

The entire coastal section of this route is fairly well waymarked, forming part of the South West Coast Path. As a National Trail, the SWCP signage carries the acorn logo. Signs may also include coloured arrows or the words 'footpath', 'bridleway' or 'byway' to indicate which types of usage are allowed on that particular stretch. Yellow arrows indicate a Public Footpath that can be used only by walkers. Blue arrows denote a Public Bridleway which can be used by walkers, horse-riders and cyclists. A red or black arrow indicates a Public Byway – open to walkers, horse-riders, cyclists, carriage drivers and motorised vehicles.

The direction indicated by the arrow is usually obvious. If in doubt, assess its direction while looking straight at the arrow. Beware of side routes, sometimes marked with arrows on the sides of the SWCP post, in tempting yellow: unless the acorn icon is also present, do not follow them.

Despite the route's good waymarking, if you have a GPS-enabled smartphone or receiver, then take it along: see page 71 for more, including how to download our file. It may be handy for finding off-route lodgings and for avoiding becoming lost in mist or fog.

> *i* **Scallops and pilgrims**
> The scallop sign is most often seen on the Route of St James (Santiago de Compostela). Its origin is in the posthumous miracle that is credited to St James. After he was beheaded in Jerusalem (in AD 44), James' body was returned to Galicia in Spain. As the boat bearing his body approached the coast, a horse on a clifftop bolted and plummeted into the Atlantic with its rider on its back. St James intervened to save the knight and his horse, who emerged from the sea alive, covered in scallop shells.

St Michael's Way combines rural and village lanes and byways marked by posts and fingerposts that display the scalloped shell often carried by pilgrims. To avoid frustration, consider using a GPS device to help navigate the fields and obscure turnings: waymarks are mysteriously sparse across some farmland parts.

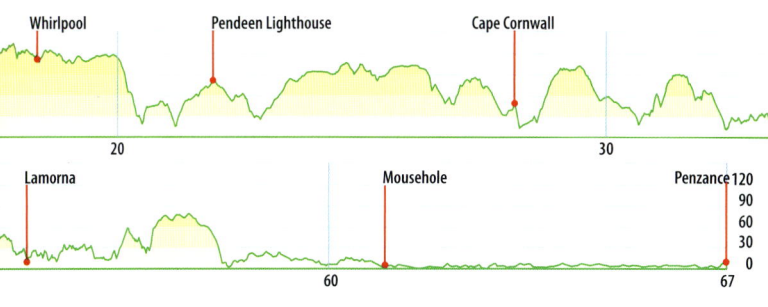

Buses in western Cornwall

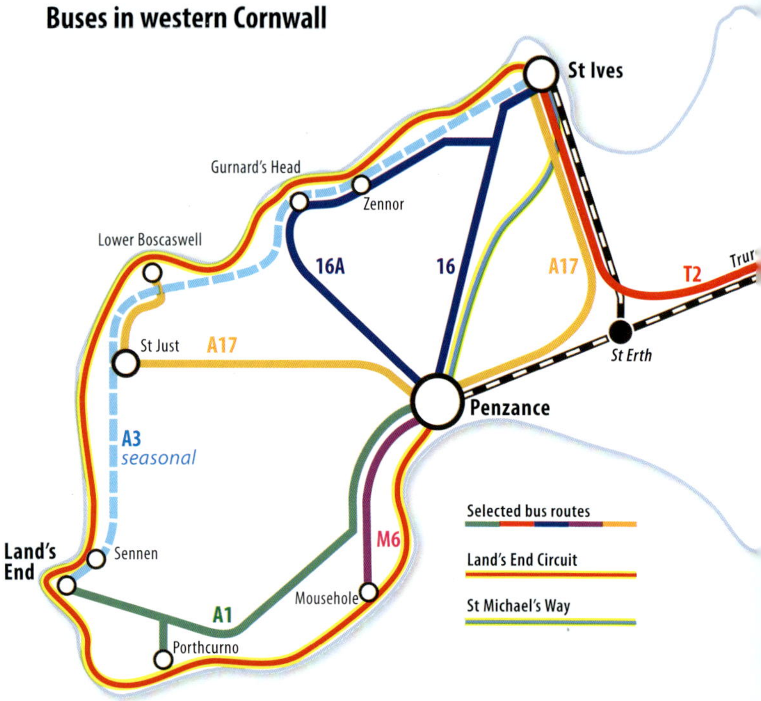

Local bus routes link places near the route. The bus company Kernow (whose name means Cornwall in the Cornish language) provides a range of services including the A1, A17, M6 and 16A (year-round), and the coastal A3 which is seasonal: see the map above.

There are links to all relevant providers and their timetables on page 71.

Countryside Code and safety

Take care of the countryside that you walk through, and try to minimise disturbance to the residents, to farming and to local activities. Know and respect the Countryside Code as promoted by Natural England: see panel. Avoid disturbing farm animals or wildlife – walk around cattle not among them, and keep well away if they have calves.

If walking with a dog, be aware that they are not permitted on many beaches except out of season. Your dog must always be under close control and you need to pick up its mess, and dispose of it suitably. Give cattle an especially wide berth if a dog is with you, and monitor their reaction carefully. If they respond aggressively, you are at serious risk and should let the dog off the lead, escaping the field by the shortest, fastest route. Take utmost care to avoid this situation. Remember also that having your dog will create many constraints over where you can eat and, crucially, for your overnight accommodation.

As with any multi-day hike, you are responsible for your own safety and should ensure you wear or carry suitable clothing and footwear for whatever weather and terrain you may face. Check the weather forecast before you set off and review each section to ensure you are fit enough to complete it within the time and daylight that is available. Find out if there are options for escape or shortcuts. Tell someone where you are going and what time you are likely to confirm your arrival or return.

Carry enough to eat and drink for your needs: it is unsafe to drink from streams or surface water unless you filter or purify. Take adequate sun protection: sea breezes make sunburn more likely.

This challenging coastal walk has remote, exposed sections and requires precautions beyond the above:

> **Countryside Code**
> **Respect other people**
> Consider the local community and other people enjoying the outdoors
> Leave gates and property as you find them and follow paths unless wider access is available
> **Protect the natural environment**
> Leave no trace of your visit and take your litter home
> Keep dogs under effective control
> **Enjoy the outdoors**
> Plan ahead and be prepared
> Follow advice and local signs
> Download the leaflet from
> **www.naturalengland.org.uk**.

- Don't be deceived by modest distances: the trail undulates constantly and walking into the wind is tiring.
- Keep yourself, children and dogs well away from cliff edges which may be crumbling or overhanging. Fog and high winds are more likely on coastal cliff-tops.
- If you are tempted by side paths that lead steeply down to coves, avoid descending unless certain that you can get back up.
- Cross a beach only if you know the tide times and can be confident you will not be cut off.
- If possible, carry a GPS device with backup battery power.
- In an emergency dial 999 or 112 and ask for the coastguard, but be aware that mobile (cellphone) coverage is patchy.

Packing checklist

Essential
- comfortable, waterproof walking boots
- specialist walking socks
- breathable clothing in layers
- waterproof jacket and overtrousers
- sun hat and sunglasses
- guidebook and compass
- whistle and torch for attracting attention in case of injury
- water carrier and plenty of water (up to 3 litres per day)
- enough food to last between supply points
- first aid kit including blister treatment
- toiletries and overnight necessities
- insect repellent and sun protection (summer)
- rucksack (at least 30 litres)
- waterproof rucksack cover and/or liner e.g., bin liner (garbage bag)
- enough cash in pounds sterling, with credit or debit card as backup
- credit cards are not always accepted and there are almost no cash machines along the trail. Bin bags have many uses e.g. to store wet clothing, or prevent hypothermia.

Desirable
- walking pole(s)
- binoculars: useful for navigation and spotting wildlife
- camera (ideally light and rugged)
- spare camera batteries and memory cards
- mains charger and adaptor (if needed)
- GPS-enabled smartphone or receiver: see page 71
- pouch or secure pockets, to keep small items handy but safe
- gaiters
- toilet tissue (biodegradable)
- small plastic bags for litter
- spare socks: changing socks at lunchtime can relieve damp feet
- towel and sink-plug
- spare lightweight shoes (e.g. crocs, trainers or sandals)
- notebook and pen.

> A mobile phone is useful for making arrangements but **don't rely on one for emergencies.**

Camping

If you are camping you need much more gear, including a tent, sleeping gear, camping stove, fuel, cooking utensils and food. Your rucksack will need to be larger e.g. 50-80 litres; and camping could add 5 to 10 kg or more to your pack weight. Previous experience is advisable. Note you have no right to wild camp unless you have obtained permission from the relevant landowner.

Cornish language, placenames and pronunciation

The Cornish language is one of the Brythonic (British) branches of the Celtic languages, closely related to Welsh and Breton, and less closely to Irish and Scots Gaelic, and Manx. It started to diverge from Welsh some time from the late 7th century. Old Cornish was used from about 800-1250 AD. Some literature in Middle Cornish survives from the period 1250-1550. Late or Modern Cornish went into steep decline during the 19th century and the last known speaker, John Mann, died in 1914.

The 20th century saw attempts at a revival, sometimes dated from the publication of Henry Jenner's handbook in 1904. Later in the 20th century, various factions became entrenched over different spelling systems. The Cornish Language Partnership has tried to resolve the issue with a standard written form, agreed in 2008. In recent years there has been a revival of interest, especially in relation to folk music, poetry, broadcasting and the arts.

The number of speakers increased sixfold between 1980 and 2000, with fluent speakers then estimated at 300. The number of Cornish residents who know some greetings and phrases is vastly higher than that, and Cornish names are popular for houses and pets. The language is taught at some schools and at Exeter University. Cornwall Council maintains a Cornish Language Office which promotes the language: see page 71.

Learning at least a few words will help you to understand many placenames. Richard Carew's *Survey of Cornwall* (1602) included the famous rhyming verse:

By *tre*, *pol*, and *pen*
Shall ye know all Cornishmen

which you can decode using the Cornish below. You will find many other clues to placenames. A rough guide to pronunciation follows.

Vocabulary guide

du	black
enys	island
gwynn	white
hal	cliff
nans	valley
pen	headland
pol	pool
pons	bridge
porth	bay
tre	homestead
wheal	mine

Pronunciation guide

Botallack	buh-**tal**-ick
Geevor	rhymes with *geezer*
Levant	le-**vant**
Ludgvan	ludge-ven
Maen	mane
Marazion	marraz-**eye**-un
Minack	min-ack
Mousehole	**mao**-zul
Nanjizal	nan-**zid**-jal
Penzance	pen-**zance**
Tater	**tay**-ter

2.1 Landscape and its formation

Cornwall's rich geological heritage is the key to understanding its fretted cliffs, hidden coves, impressive wildlife and its economic heritage of fishing and mining. Geographers know the Land's End peninsula as Penwith, from the Cornish words *pen* (headland) and *wydh* (at the end).

This most westerly headland of mainland Britain is a granite rampart jutting out into the Atlantic, and was the last piece of the island to be created. The tectonic plates bearing England and Scotland collided about 500 million years ago. This was the biggest nation-building event in Britain's history, but Cornwall was still not on the map.

Around 100 million years later Britain – which was part of the Laurentian plate – was approached from the south by the Gondwanaland plate. As these two plates converged, the ocean between them was squeezed. Land and sea-floor were pushed upwards, just as the Himalaya were later created when India collided with Asia. Finally, at the extreme south-west of England, Cornwall was born. Lizard Point, south-east of our route, has an *ophiolite* – a relic of ocean floor that was trapped like a finger in the closing tectonic window.

Movements of this magnitude caused cracks in the earth's crust. Boiling magma welled up later, eventually to cool and crystallise as the granites of the 'Cornubian Batholith' – *Cornubia* is medieval Latin for Cornwall and *batholith* refers to a large mass of rock pushed up from the molten magma to crystallise above ground. At first, Cornwall's high mountains probably stood up to 3000 m (9850 ft) tall.

Land's End from the west

Eventually erosion wore down the mountains to the undulating plateau that we see today, much of it at around 130 m (425 ft) above sea level with a high point of 252 m (825 ft). Underground, however, the molten magma persisted for a long time. This meant that the rocks cooled slowly, so the crystals of granite were large. In addition, radiant heat baked the surrounding land. This caused a wide range of changes to the neighbouring 'country rock', creating tin, tungsten, copper, other minerals and clay. By about 250 million years ago, much of this metamorphism was complete.

The following eras saw more change and upheaval. Further magma was injected intermittently. Sediments were deposited as this region was submerged and uplifted – sometimes in desert equatorial latitudes and at other times outside this band. Final sculpting was wrought by wind and water. The granites were eventually exposed in places, most recently by the fringes of Ice Age activity that ended about 12,000 years ago, and most vividly in the exposure of the massive tors on top of hills. A *tor* is an exposed rock formation – often one that has been weathered into strangely shaped blocks.

Ice Ages also played havoc with sea levels, leading for example to 'raised beaches'. Waves cut level platforms that, after sea levels fell, became dry land. Erosion also ate into small cracks in the rocks, enlarging them, and eventually causing sea cliffs to fail. This left hidden coves that over time filled with sand, strange sea stacks such as the Armed Knight and arches such as Enys Dodnan: see pages 46-7 for a photo.

The Royal Geological Society of Cornwall was founded in 1814, only seven years after the Geological Society of London. That Cornwall hosted the world's second such association underscores the importance of its geology.

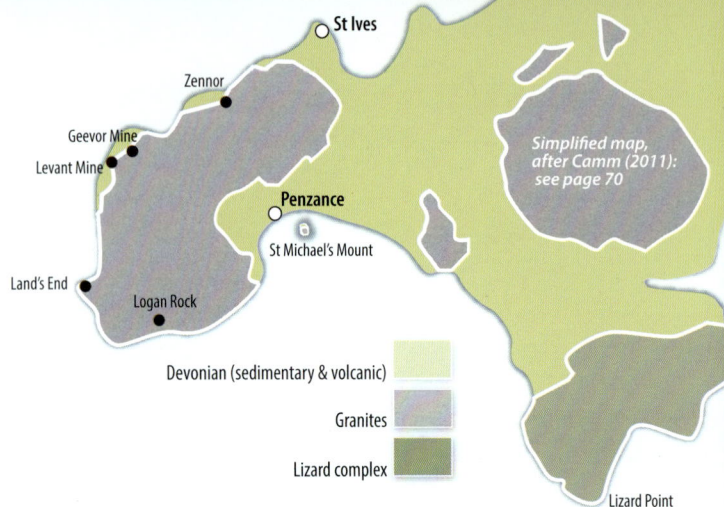

Logan Rock

Top geological sights along the coast include:

- tin mines such as Geevor Mine (in granite) and Levant Mine (in sedimentary and volcanic rocks)
- huge boulders such as Logan Rock, near Treen, a 80-ton granite boulder that can be rocked, but not toppled, by a single person: *logan* means rocking stone
- raised beaches such as Porth Nanven, near St Just
- anthropomorphic shapes in the rocks at Land's End
- intruded granite sheets that can be seen cutting through the cliffs where the cove has exposed them at Wicca Pool, near Zennor
- pillow-lavas that originally erupted over marine sediments, and metamorphosed into a hard greenstone that resists weathering and thus often makes up headlands – e.g. at Clodgy Point and Gurnard's Head
- granite outcrops covered with sediments on the landward side at St Michael's Mount.

Granite intrusions at Wicca Pool

2·2 History of Cornwall

Cornwall's best preserved quoit: Trethevy

Traders, smugglers, pirates, miners, pilgrims, writers, artists, holidaymakers and now digital nomads – over the millennia, all have left their mark on Cornwall's history.

Ancient hunter-gatherers of Neolithic tribes settled here, having crossed from continental Europe about 10,000 years ago. Their presence remains through their flints, arrowheads and capstoned tombs, known as quoits – e.g. near Zennor). Later Bronze Age tribes left stone circles. These are typically 1-2 km inland from the coastal route – e.g. Merry Maidens of Boleigh, near Lamorna – a stone circle dating from 2500-1500 BC.

The Celts arrived around 500 BC, bringing iron tools and weapons, and leaving hill forts such as Chyauster, 4 km off-route near Treen. The Celts also left their legacy in the names of places and people: see page 15.

The Roman occupation and the Dark Ages of Angle, Saxon and Danish invasions led to the Arthurian legends with their links to Tintagel Castle further up the Cornish coast. Pilgrimage links developed between Ireland, Wales, England and Brittany, including St Michael's Way. And from about the 8th century, St Michael's Mount developed as a monastery.

The Norman era and Middle Ages saw Cornwall's economy develop in farming, fishing, and mining. By the early 19th century, Devon and Cornwall would come to dominate the global market for tin: see pages 21 to 22.

Cornwall's smuggling industry grew in parallel. The English government began imposing customs duties to meet the growing demands of financing military action. From 1275 onwards these levies extended from wool to gin, tea and other products. Beneath this price umbrella, a whole system soon developed whereby ships were lured by false lights so they would founder on rocks and could be plundered by the locals. This allowed the contraband to be sold easily, tax-free and well below market rates, with the connivance of the entire community – even the vicar.

Smuggling reached its peak in the late 18th century. But the industry became too conspicuous and, after the murder of a customs official, 'coast guards' were eventually established to guard against smuggling. They developed cliff-top lookouts and the pathways that would eventually become the SWCP.

Shipwreck at Boscawen Cove

During the 15th and 16th centuries, Britain strengthened its maritime presence. Naval leaders included famous sons of neighbouring Devon such as Drake and Raleigh. Although the Spanish Armada of 1588 was seen off, subsequent raids saw Mousehole and Penzance sacked, as remembered in the name of nearby Point Spaniard.

The 17th through to 19th centuries allowed Cornwall to prosper while a combination of capital and innovation fuelled an industrial revolution in mining technology. It achieved global dominance in tin mining but was eventually undercut by cheaper foreign products. By the mid-19th century, its mining was ruined: see page 22.

Early tourism started to fill the gap left by mining. The Napoleonic Wars of 1803–1815 put Europe in lock-down, so the Grand Tourists travelled within Britain instead. The south coast climate was attractive, and after the railway arrived in 1859 it also became accessible.

Tourism increased throughout the 20th century, with the opening of nearby National Parks, the promotion of Areas of Outstanding Natural Beauty, the 'draw' of famous writers and artists in residence such as Agatha Christie, Daphne Du Maurier, D H Lawrence and Barbara Hepworth, and the development of initiatives such as Tate St Ives and the Eden Project. But the economic impact of the arrival of lifestyle-seeking digital nomads has barely balanced the decline of mining and the pressures on the fishing industry.

2·3 Mining

Cornwall was renowned for its tin as long ago as the Bronze Age. Analysis of the 'Nebra sky disc', the 12-inch metal plate shown here, reveals that Cornish gold and tin was in use by about 1600 BC. Found near Mittelberg, Germany in 1999, this bronze-and-gold disc is the world's oldest depiction of the cosmos and its celestial bodies.

In addition, St Michael's Mount has been identified as a possible site of Ictis, a port whence tin was exported, mentioned by the historian Diodorus Siculus in the first century BC. An important strand of Celtic legend portrays Joseph of Arimathea as a tin trader who brought the infant Jesus to Cornwall.

After centuries of smaller-scale extraction, Cornwall eventually became global leader in tin, copper and other minerals in the 18th and early 19th centuries. This boom was driven by three factors:
- demand for minerals and metals triggered by the industrial revolution (c1760-1820)
- the availability of finance including from abroad, and
- innovation in the techniques of extraction and refining.

Aerial view of Levant mine with winding engine in foreground

The beam engine was one of those innovations. This was a new way to pump water from the mines that are close to the sea, and sometimes even from beneath it. Others included the Davy Lamp to warn of methane in mines, developed by Cornishman Humphry Davy (1778–1829): see pages 58-9.

By 1837 Cornwall had 200 mines, employing 30,000 workers. Many of these were children, and all miners faced danger and received poor wages for hard work in unpleasant conditions. Most workers followed the Methodist faith of John Wesley (1703-1791), a denomination that started hereabouts. The mining legacy survives in the UNESCO World Heritage Site Cornwall and West Devon Mining Landscape. Prime examples include Botallack's windswept Crowns Mine, and Levant Mine with its deep undersea workings and reconstructed beam engine. Geevor was the last working mine in the area, producing large quantities of tin and copper, and closed as late as 1991. It is cared for by Pendeen Community Heritage, a charity formed in 2000 that offers interpretation and experiences including a guided underground tour. Its Museum and Heritage Centre is on the outskirts of Pendeen: **www.geevor.com**.

Engine house, Levant (built in 1887)

By the mid-19th century, the industry had started its decline. Lodes were becoming harder to reach, and prices were dropping as mines in Australia, Mexico and the USA came onstream at lower cost. A third of Cornwall's mining families emigrated – often to ply their trade at mines abroad.

Fans of the BBC's Poldark saga will recognise many of its locations as they walk the route. Dramatising many of the themes mentioned above, the series features locations such as Levant Mine, Crowns Mine, Porthcurno and Porthgwarra. Here is a Poldark-themed driving route **www.intocornwall.com**.

Levant arsenic works, Geevor

2·4 Habitats and wildlife

Peregrine falcon

The call of the gull, the dive of the falcon, the plunge of the dolphin and the dance of the butterfly – these are some of the wonderful wildlife experiences offered by the coastline of the Land's End peninsula.

One might expect the peninsula to have poor soils and habitats. After all, it's made primarily of hard granite, and its west and north-west facing coastlines are continually battered by Atlantic wind and brine. But the warm sea current and the area's southerly latitude lead to a relatively mild climate; there are just enough sedimentary and metamorphic rocks to provide sufficient nutrients; and the coves of its south-facing coast are well-sheltered and face the sun.

As a result, the area is ecologically important: excluding the last 3 miles/5 km of the walk, the entire coastline is protected as an Area of Outstanding Natural Beauty. Most of the route passes through Sites of Special Scientific Interest (SSSIs).

Bottlenose dolphin

Bird life

Cornwall has huge avian diversity: the Cornish Red Data Book records 462 species of bird across Cornwall and the Scilly Isles. Located at the south-western tip of the British mainland, the peninsula is an important resting and feeding area for migratory birds, especially in sheltered valleys.

Gannet

Peregrine falcons and ravens nest on secluded cliff slopes and crags. You might spot a falcon in a high-speed dive or 'stoop': it preys mainly on pigeons and other birds which it catches on the wing. It is by far the fastest bird in the world, achieving speeds of well over 180 mph (290 kph). Special baffles in its nostrils allow it to breathe at extreme velocity. In Cornish dialect, falcons are known as 'winnards' and local expressions include 'shrammed as a winnard' (meaning deeply chilled).

Cliff ledges provide nesting sites for seabirds including fulmars, shags, kittiwakes and gulls. Areas of scrub on the cliff-tops and in the valleys provide nesting sites for many species including stonechats and warblers. For Porthgwarra alone, the SSSI citation includes 186 species of bird that are resident, over-wintering or passing through, including the ubiquitous gulls and

Chough

skuas, stonechats, whitethroats, chiffchaffs and peregrine falcons.

In several places including Gwennap Head, you may see choughs. These red-billed, red-legged members of the crow family have been beloved of the Cornish for centuries, and they feature on Cornwall's coat of arms. The chough came under pressure from the late 18th century when more intensive farming started to destroy its natural habitat of cropped grassland. The population was finally reduced to a single pair nesting near Newquay, of which the last bird died in 1973. Happily, 28 years later a pair settled on the Lizard Peninsula, and since 2001 they have bred successfully. The chough population has since grown and spread further across Cornwall.

Stonechat on gorse

Nearer the waterline – including at the RSPB-managed sanctuaries of Hayle Estuary, a few kilometres from St Ives, and at Marazion Marsh – you will sight gannets, guillemots, manx shearwaters, curlews, little egrets, oystercatchers, cormorants and shags. The wide variety of duck species includes teal and wigeon. Visit the RSPB Discovery Centre at Land's End and use the telescopes to see gannets diving for fish at breakneck speeds, plunging into the water at up to 62 mph/100 kph.

Oystercatchers

Butterflies

Butterflies have a special affinity with Cornwall's temperate climate, and are there are 38 species. More common varieties include red admiral, small tortoiseshell, painted lady and hedge brown. Rarer species include the small copper, gatekeeper, common blue, silver studded blue, silver-washed fritillary and dark green fritillary.

Some species such as silver-studded blue feed as larvae on a variety of plants such as gorse, bell heather, and cross-leaved heath, to emerge in June and survive until August. Others such as the migrant red admiral may be seen on warm days year-round. The painted lady is another migrant, unable to survive winter in the UK. It travels from North Africa, the Middle East and southern Europe during the summer – some years in large numbers.

Small copper

Left: *Common blue (male)*; below: *Painted lady*

Land animals

Otter on river bank

Moor and heathland are home to foxes (especially since the hunting ban), badgers, hares and rabbits. Various bats are found, including greater horseshoe, pipistrelle and Daubenton's bat; disused mines are a favourite haunt. Adders (Britain's only venomous snake), other snakes and slow worms (which are legless lizards) can be found on exposed moor and heathland. The otter is returning to selected river banks.

Fox

Marine life

Cornwall's marine life is also diverse. Bottlenose dolphin (and the rarer Risso's dolphin) and porpoise live in family groups with territories that range over hundreds of miles, so it is hard to predict where sightings will be made – but Land's End, Sennen Cove, Cape Cornwall and Mount's Bay are good options. Also consider taking a viewing trip by boat from Penzance.

Grey seals breed on the coast between Clodgy Point and Gurnard's Head, and sometimes haul out on the Carracks and other offshore islets. They can be seen basking in the sun in remote coves. Britain is home to about 40% of the world's grey seals, which thrive around the Cornish coast. In Cornwall, the so-called common seal is an uncommon sight, but recent sightings suggest their population may be recovering. Grey seals are easily distinguished from common (harbour) seals by their longer, straighter snouts set in a larger head, whereas common seals have rounder faces with V-shaped nostrils.

Grey seal (female)

Other larger animals include the basking shark, often sighted in summer as they follow the warm current up Britain's west coast: this is the North Atlantic Drift which has its origins in the Gulf of Mexico. The basking shark is one of the world's largest fish, second only to the whale shark. Typically adults are about 8 m (26 ft) long, though the largest ever recorded accurately was 12 m (40 ft). Their life expectancy is about 50 years and they can give birth only once every 2-4 years. Feeding on zooplankton, they can filter up to 1500 cubic metres of seawater per hour.

Plant life

Large areas of moorland and heath are enlivened by vivid yellow gorse from January to June, by pink or purple sea thrift in late spring or summer and by purple heather from summer onwards. Common gorse is the more widespread variety, whereas western gorse has a lower growth habit. Both are long-flowering and provide important nectar for invertebrates and shelter for birds.

The cliffs and tops are home to an intricate variety of habitats. The cliff faces support a rocky maritime community including thrift, rock samphire, sea aster and sea spleenwort. Among the cliff faces, rock ledges support maritime plants known as *therophyte* – annual plants that complete their life cycle rapidly whenever conditions are favourable. These include thrift, stonecrop, kidney vetch and buck's-horn plantain.

Sea buckthorn

Higher up, the cliff slopes and tops consist of maritime grassland, heath and scrub. The cliff grassland is dominated by perennial Yorkshire fog grass and red fescue which often forms a thick sward. Thrift, wild carrots, sea campions, sea plantains and oxeye daisies are common. Bluebells are sometimes found in more sheltered areas and on upper slopes.

Scrubland communities of plants, including stands of bracken, occur on the cliffs and particularly in the valleys. Common gorse, bramble and sea blackthorn are frequent, associated with cock's-foot and bluebells. Where the cliffs are more sheltered and face predominantly south – between Gwennap Head and Carn-du – plant growth is stronger so that bushes, bracken, hedges and trees become taller and thicker.

Thrift on Cornish clifftop

St Ives

North over St Ives harbour

The origin and name of St Ives are attributed to the 5th-century Irish missionary Saint Ia. From medieval times the town was one of the most important fishing ports in Cornwall. Its narrow, cobbled streets and tiny houses are places where nets were once mended, pilchards packed, and preparations made for export to the continent. The original 15th-century pier was replaced (1766-70) by one designed by John Smeaton – a pioneering civil engineer who re-discovered cement that could set underwater. The pier's octagonal lookout was the original lighthouse, augmented by the newer one visible on the now-lengthened pier.

The Great Western Railway was extended from St Erth in 1877, bringing accessibility and tourism. Bars, restaurants and art galleries arrived, then surfers and sunbathers on the award-winning beaches of Porthmeor and Porthminster. Major attractions include Tate St Ives (its contemporary space dedicated to artists with a Cornish connection), the Barbara Hepworth Museum (former home of the leading abstract sculptor), the eclectic St Ives Museum on Wheal Dream and St Ia's harbourside church. For opening hours and more, visit our *Route links* page as explained on page 70.

North-west over Carbis Bay to St Ives Head

3.1 St Ives to Zennor Head

Distance	7·2 miles 11·6 km
Terrain	mostly good paths with several rough parts – occasional need for hands; several sections boggy
Grade	flat in St Ives, then undulating; ascent helped by granite block steps on steepest sections; altitude gain 450 m, loss 390 m
Food and drink	Trevalgan caravan site and Treveal Farm both 1 km offroute, Tremedda Farm barely offroute
Summary	a spectacular introduction to the SWCP; rugged granite cliffs, wide sea vistas, high moors and heaths; remote Zennor (offroute) worth visiting

```
0·0              2·5                                 4·7                      7·
○────────────────●───────────────●───────────────────●────────────────────────○
St Ives          4·1         Carn Naun Point         7·5                 Zennor Hea
station
```

- From the train station, immediately cross the car park heading to the coast. Descend a flight of steps and turn left to join the SWCP as it heads north on a shore-hugging road called The Warren.
- About 200 m from the station, at a fork with Westcotts Quay, bear right to join Pednolva Walk. Continue for 100 m and once you reach West Pier on your right, go straight on to Wharf Road.
- Continue around the harbour onto Quay Street, to the junction with Smeaton's Pier with its lighthouse. At low tide you can instead cross the harbour on sand if you prefer. You can also visit the lighthouse.
- At the end of Quay Street, turn left onto Wheal Dream and follow it to the St Ives Museum.
- Continue on the SWCP (with waymarks occasional) around the coastal edge of a large car park beside Porthgwidden Beach. Go ahead to reach St Ives Head with its National Coastwatch Lookout: see photo on page 67.
- On the hill to your left stands St Nicholas Chapel which you can detour to visit, rejoining the SWCP afterwards. Continue hugging the coast around the headland, going past the Tate St Ives on your left with Porthmeor Beach on your right.

North-east across St Ives Harbour

- At the end of the beach, 250 m past the Tate, spot a bowling green and be sure to skirt it closely, keeping it on your right.

    If travelling clockwise: from the bowling green, emerge onto Beach Road on your right, and continue in the clear direction towards St Ives.
- The path is now tarmac, and then grass. Head straight on for 30 m, then after 25 m swing left on the path as you pass a shelter on your right.

Boat at St Ives Harbour

- After a gentle uphill then downhill, reach a more sustained incline that climbs 50 m over a 1 km stretch. After some stones and boulders, reach Clodgy Point: a sign on a low granite block indicates this is an Area of Outstanding Natural Beauty.

- From here all the way until Mousehole (near Penzance), paths may tempt you to right and left. Stay on the main path by remaining alert to waymarks, with the general aim of keeping near to the coast but not too close.

- Continue for 1 km to reach Hor Point, where the path runs about 20 m inland from the cliff edge: ignore the path that heads down to your right unless you wish to incur the extra 50 m of descent and ascent.

- The path dips slightly then climbs to reach Pen Enys Point; detour here for good views around the head of the point 30 m to your right, though you may need to fight through undergrowth.

Marker near start of path

- Over the next 1 km pass a sign to Trevalgan Touring Park (about 1 km inland), then a beach and three small coves far below. Finally, with the help of two boardwalks, reach Carn Naun Point.
- Here the path again cuts across the headland as you pass a trig point on your left. (As of 2019, a diversion took you further inland on a brief signed detour.) You are now slightly over half-way to Zennor Head, and on a clear day Pendeen Watch (lighthouse) is visible 11 km further on.
- Follow the path as it swings south-west and descends steeply towards River Cove. The path doglegs right then left before it crosses the small footbridge, then zigzags left and right before starting a brief climb to reach a low green National Trust sign for Treveal – a large area that includes Iron Age and other heritage sites.

Marker en route to Zennor

Headland on the way to Zennor

- Pass the Carracks, large offshore islands on which seals may be basking, and continue uphill past Economy Cove to reach Mussel Point. You are now about 2 km beyond the trig point on Carn Naun.
- Follow the path south for about 500 m along the cliff-tops above Wicca Pool. Here granite was mined and shipped to St Ives in the early 1400s to build St Ia's church, and the novelist D H Lawrence (who lived at Higher Tregerthen) swam nearby.

Marker at the optional turn-off to Zennor

- The path now swings east and a low green sign informs that you are on Tregerthen Cliff; the site was acquired by the National Trust in 1962, paid for by local subscription.
- The promontory of Zennor Head is now clearly visible ahead, reached by 2 km of undulating path. The rocky headland is barely 10 m off-route, so it is easy to explore and/or to shelter there.
- Stay on the path as it turns to rise south-west for 20 m, and at weathered granite tors turns south-east, rising steeply to a junction – a climb of 5 m over 30 m.

- Here the SWCP turns 90° right at a low granite National Trust sign, but if you are staying in Zennor, instead head straight on for 500 m.

  If travelling clockwise: ensure you turn left at this junction, or turn right if you are staying at Zennor.

- At Zennor, you can stay in the Tinners Arms or a local B&B. Explore the local church with its mermaid chair and fable. Impressive Neolithic sites are about a mile away uphill, so may require a longer stay.

- With the stone gateway that marks the way to Zennor in front of you, turn right at the low granite sign.

Church at Zennor

3·2 Zennor Head to the Crowns

Distance	9·1 miles 14·7 km
Terrain	mostly good paths; some stretches need care – generally avoid scrambly rocks lower down
Grade	many undulations up to cliff-tops and down to coves, especially during the first half, with some level stretches later; altitude gain 560 m, loss 595 m
Food and drink	Treen and Pendeen 1-2 km offroute
Summary	craggy cliffs and broad cliff-tops eventually bring you to the landmark of Pendeen Watch (lighthouse) and to a superb introduction to the tin mines beyond

7·2 — Zennor Head — 3·4 — 2·1 — Gurnard's Head — 1·6 — 1·0 — Porthmeor Cove — 3·9 — 6·3 — Pendeen Watch — 3·4 — 2·1 — The Crowns — 16

- Descend two flights of stone steps, cross a footbridge over a stream, then zigzag to the top of the next rise. Keep a short wall to your left before dipping down northward then uphill southward again.
- Pass a ruin on your right, then skirt Porthglaze Cove quite close to its sheer cliffs.
- Continue for 1 km over several step-assisted undulations, crossing two footbridges. You will see Gurnard's Head extending to your right – an optional 1-km detour. A path to your left would take you to Gurnard's Head Hotel and Treen, for refreshment or accommodation.
- Continue for 1·5 km with a short rise, then head largely downhill to Porthmeor Cove. After good views backwards to Gurnard's Head, you reach a slab-bridge.
- Continue mainly uphill for 1·4 km to reach Bosigran Cliff, popular with climbers; notice to your immediate right the vestiges of an Iron Age hill fort.

The slab-bridge

Pendeen Lighthouse coming into view

- Follow the path south-west for 1 km to reach stepping stones, Whirl Pool Bay and Trevean Cliff. En route, stay aware of your general compass direction to avoid side tracks: the path is indistinct and waymarks are few.
- Bear east along the path for 3 km to reach the lighthouse at Pendeen Watch with the help of a footbridge, steps, and eventually a track to the car park. The lighthouse was built in 1891, and automated in 1995. It now offers holiday-let cottages.
- Leave the car park on the tarmac track that leads south, and after 300 m pass three houses on your left. Opposite the last house follow an indistinct sign on your right to join a footpath.

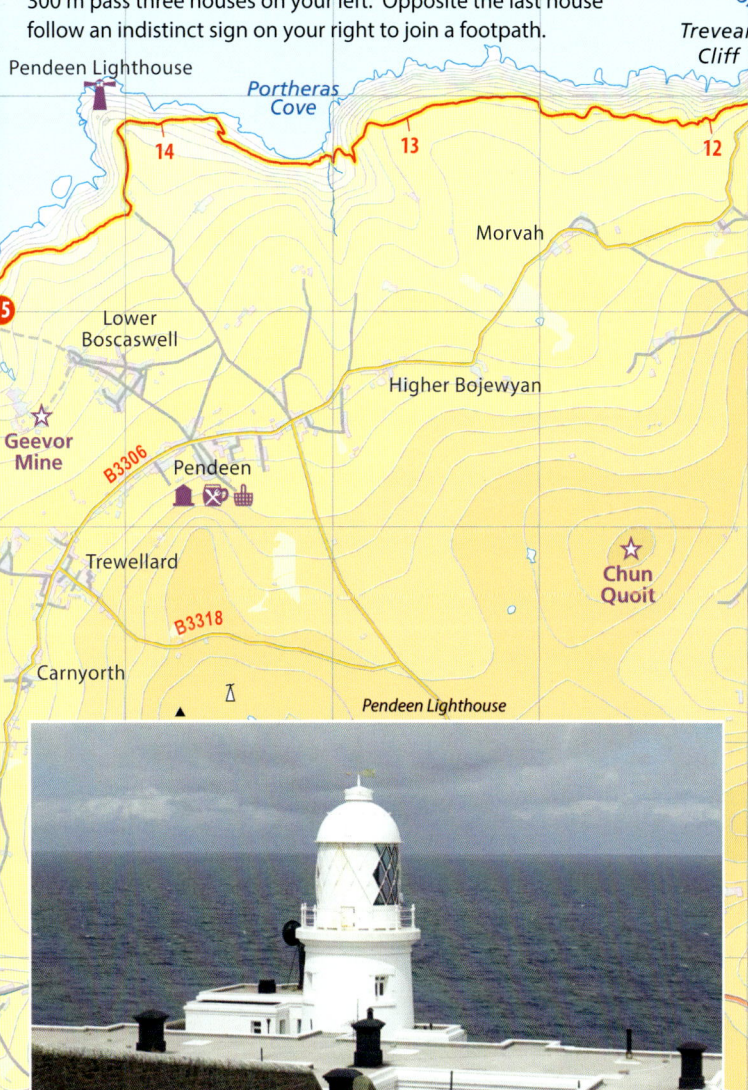

Pendeen Lighthouse

Copper leaching down the cliff, Trewellard Bottoms

- ⚠ The path soon re-joins the coast, and mine buildings now become apparent, especially as you reach Trewellard Bottoms 1 km after where you left the tarmac. Visible high on your left is a classic winching wheel at Geevor Mine, 500 m off-route, but with a guided exhibition of Cornish mining.
- Pendeen (with facilities) lies 1 km away via a path that lies fractionally to the north of the path to Geevor, passing through Lower Boscaswell.
- Continue gently uphill following waymarks through the mining remains that include a calciner – a chamber where valuable arsenic was condensed onto the walls and scraped off by hand. After 600 m, reach Levant Mine.
- The Levant Engine House (owned by the National Trust) lies immediately adjacent to the right of the route. The site is rich in the history of mining – walk its length, or pause to take a tour.
- At the end of the site, turn left and pass through the obvious car park, exiting on the opposite side to follow the SWCP beside a wall of large stones on your left.

Levant Mine

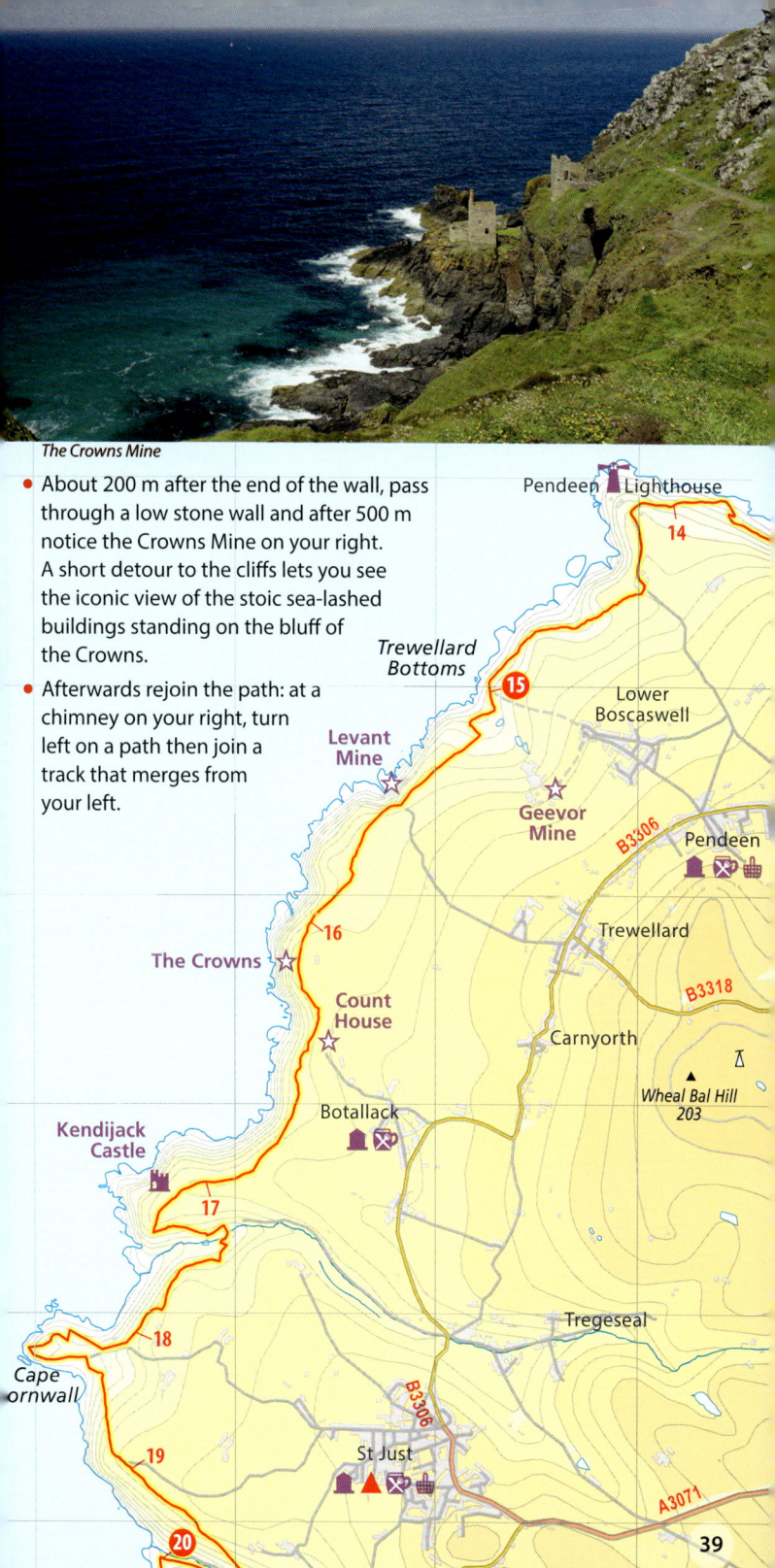

The Crowns Mine

- About 200 m after the end of the wall, pass through a low stone wall and after 500 m notice the Crowns Mine on your right. A short detour to the cliffs lets you see the iconic view of the stoic sea-lashed buildings standing on the bluff of the Crowns.

- Afterwards rejoin the path: at a chimney on your right, turn left on a path then join a track that merges from your left.

Cape Cornwall distant ahead

- ⚠ The SWCP bears right off this track after just 30 m. To detour to Botallack Count House (exhibits and refreshments), continue instead along that track for 300 m. Afterwards return westwards towards the sea to resume the SWCP.
- To reach accommodation in Botallack, continue on the track past the Count House to the Queen's Arms pub after 500 m, and Botallack's farms and caravan site soon afterwards.

3·3 The Crowns to Land's End

Distance 8·7 miles 13·9 km
Terrain mostly good paths, with short stretches on road
Grade typical gradients and undulations; altitude gain 520 m, loss 470 m
Food and drink refreshments on route at Cape Cornwall, Sennen Cove and Land's End
Summary varied and picturesque section that moves from mining landscape, via Cape Cornwall to Land's End, with its spectacular sea features

16·3	2·0		5·5		1·1	25·0
The Crowns	3·2	Cape Cornwall	8·9		Sennen Cove	1·8 Land's End
					(Harbour Car Park)	

- Fork right from the track that leads to the Count House at the Crowns, and after 100 m pass the treatment floors and arsenic calciner of Botallack Mine on your left.
- After a further 400 m, reach the remains of West Wheal Owles and Wheal Edward. Take care to avoid the many disused mine shafts in this area.
- Having joined a track for just 20 m, bear off it to the right and continue for 300 m to reach the obvious, though modest, remains of Kendijack Castle.
- The path passes the ruins to their left, but it's an easy detour to pass through them for a view of the sea on the far side: go as far as the cliff-fence, where you turn left and drop downhill to meet the path again at a stone slab-stile.
- Stay alert for the next 1 km or so because the signs are low and easily missed. From the stile drop downhill for 100 m; turn left to follow a track for 75 m; drop down again on an indicated path for 200 m; then turn left on the indicated path for a further 200 m.
- An indicated right turn takes you across a footbridge to traverse the valley, after which the path winds uphill eventually to join a track where you turn sharp right.
- The path levels and drops over the next 500 m, then you join a track and turn right as indicated, passing a long building high on your left.

Looking back over Cape Cornwall, with waymarker

- With the chimney tower atop Cape Cornwall as your guide, turn right when you reach the tarmac road that leads to the Cape's car park. Keep right to walk parallel to the road on grass, and after 120 m bear right to enter the field which has the remains of St Helen's Chapel.
- Pass through the ruins and go straight on to the north-west corner of the field. An obvious path climbs up to reach the tall chimney atop the Cape's headland.
- Descend to pass Cape Cottage, then turn right. With the car park on your left, descend steps and merge left onto a tarmac road. Follow the road for 100 m, then turn sharp right as signed to angle back towards the coast.
- The road becomes a track. Follow it in a straight line for a stiff pull uphill for 350 m, initially passing houses on each side.
- A few metres before reaching a trig point on your left, look for the low granite sign that sends you to the right, close to the sea. Take this path downhill for 1 km until it reaches a tarmac road.
- The sign suggests a left turn for Sennen, but (as of 2019) this was not part of the SWCP: turn left at that junction only if you want to reach the A30 after 500 m.

Confusing marker near sharp right turn

Sennen Cove comes into view

- Instead the SWCP turns right to angle back towards the coast, reaching a small car park after 400 m. Then turn left to cross a brook and after a short climb, join a path that merges from your right; this path comes from the YHA hostel.
- Continue uphill for 750 m, with steep climbs helped at first by steps, then by wide zigzags. At the top of this section, ignore two unmarked paths to the left: the first after 20 m would lead back to the YHA, and the second after a further 50 m to Letcha Farm.
- For the next 2 km, the path is open and easy to follow. Its undulations are gentle, and you have great views back to Cape Cornwall.

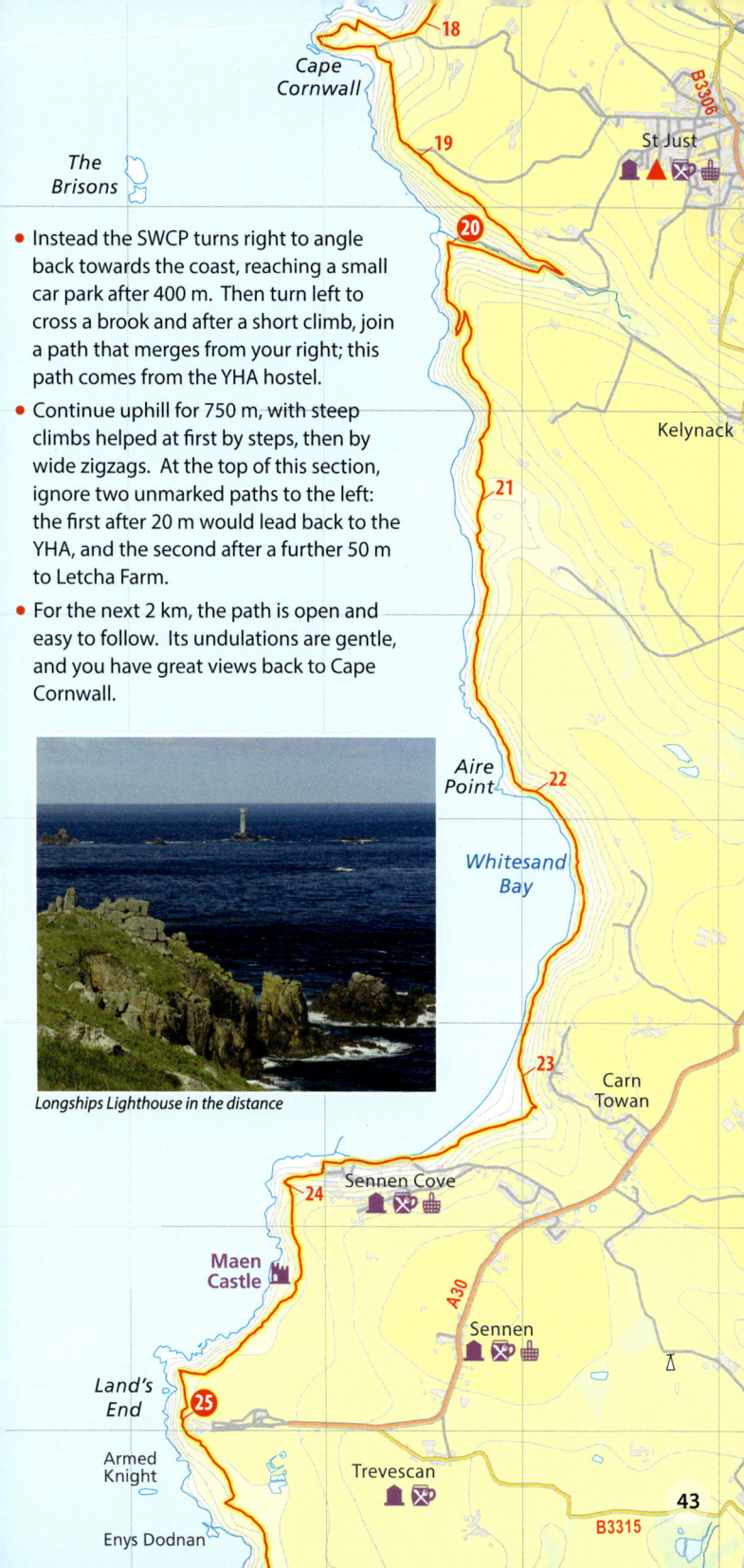

Longships Lighthouse in the distance

Sennen Cove

- After passing a bouldery shoreline below you, eventually reach several outcrops of tor-like rounded granite: you might have to use your hands to scramble through them.
- The path now extends for 2 km to reach Sennen Cove. The walking on this stretch is easy, on good paths that are gravelly, earthen and sandy or a mixture. Longships Lighthouse, 5 km off Land's End ahead, seems to draw you along.
- If you are staying in Sennen, you will need to gain the cliff-tops. They are best reached by turning left uphill on an unmarked tarmac road that crosses the SWCP before the latter dives between cottages and crosses a brook.
- The SWCP continues to the end of the beach and ascends the slipway to join the road that borders the sea.

Boats hauled out at Sennen Cove

- Follow the road for 400 m to cross a car park. Exit through its far end, turn left and go up steps ahead of you (unsigned). On the headland, reach an obvious lookout hut to your right.

Land's End Hotel

- Pass the lookout (which now displays National Trust information), and continue near the cliff-line for 150 m as indicated by a low granite sign to reach the brow of the headland. Here you can catch a glimpse of the rusting remains of RMS Mülheim, a German cargo ship wrecked on 22 March 2003. After a further 250 m a sign on the right points to the limited remains of Maen Castle, 50 m to your right. These may be worth a 15-minute exploration: see panel.

>  **Maen Castle**
> Built between 800 and 400 BC, Maen Castle may have Late Bronze Age or Neolithic origins. It may also have been occupied through Iron Age, Romano-British period, and even medieval times based on hundreds of shards of pottery found here. The stone blocks of the narrow entrance still stand, and just outside the gateway lies one of the former gate jambs, though little else remains. Of the 60 such cliff-top castles in England, 40 are in Cornwall.

- Soon after Maen Castle you gain your first view of the buildings at Land's End. Fork right towards the white-painted First and Last House (gift shop open 10.00-18.00 in summer). Go around the headland on an obvious path, passing an RSPB Discovery Centre on your right and the Land's End Hotel on your left.
- Offshore sights nearby include the Armed Knight (sea stack) and Enys Dodnan (natural arch). They appear together in the photo on pages 46-47, taken from about 800 m beyond the hotel.
- If overnighting here, double back for either the Land's End Hotel or for access to the A30 and nearby villages such as Sennen.

Land's End, with famous fingerpost

3·4 Land's End to Lamorna

48 49 51

Distance 10·4 miles 16·7 km
Terrain generally good paths
Grade typical gradients and undulations with steep steps past Minack Theatre; altitude gain 650 m, loss 725 m
Food and drink cafés at Porthgwarra and Minack Theatre; pub at Treen (offroute)
Summary a relatively long section largely on cliff-tops, with the added interest of Minack Theatre in its magical setting

25·0 — Land's End Hotel — 3·5 / 5·7 — Porthgwara — 1·3 / 2·1 — Porthcurno — 5·5 / 8·9 — Lamorna 35·4

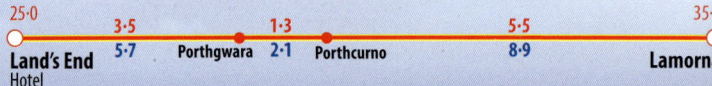

- Continue from the Land's End Hotel, passing the Armed Knight and Enys Dodnan. After a right/left dogleg at Greeb Cottage, the SWCP heads generally south-south-east, passing up and over Pordenack Point, then (1 km after Greeb Cottage) Carn Boel.
- From the top of Carn Boel, bear left (east) on a gentle descent for 300 m to reach the bay called Nanjizal.
- After 600 m reach the end of the bay and bear inland for 50 m, as signed. Turn right to cross a footbridge, then right again to climb the headland with the help of steps.

Enys Dodnan, with the Armed Knight behind, off Land's End

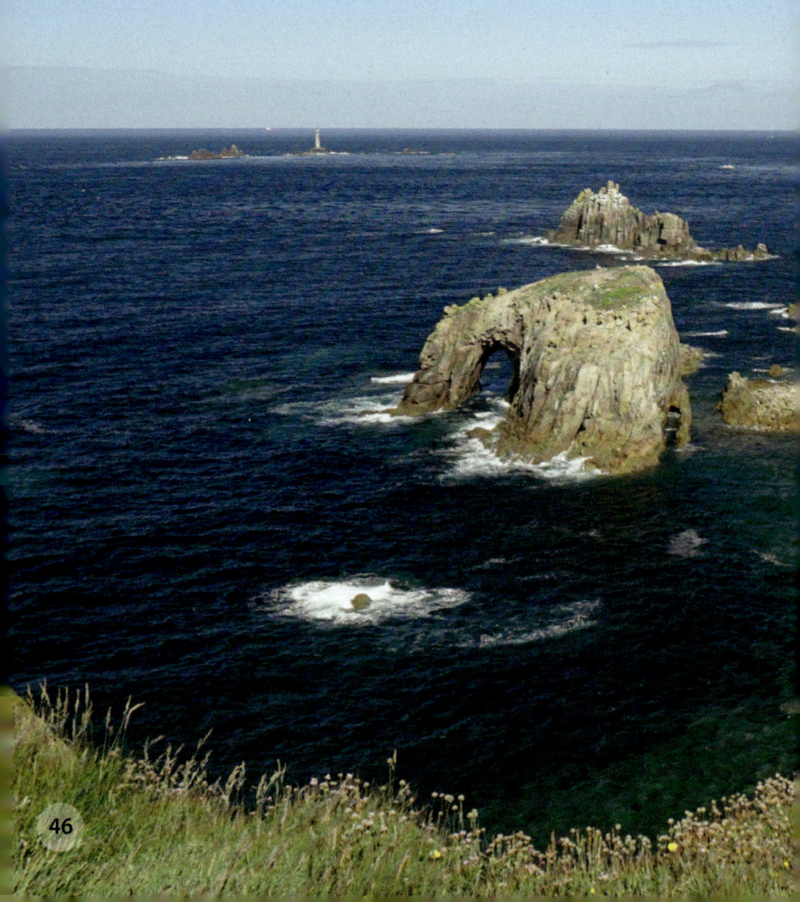

- The path is now clear, allowing relaxed striding across open headlands. After 2·5 km reach the National Coastwatch lookout at Gwennap Head, just before Porthgwarra.
- Continue on the path for 750 m, passing two huge conical daymarks (aids to ships' daytime navigation) to reach Porthgwarra (with toilets and a seasonal café).
- Continue past the cafe to cross a tarmac track, turn right as signed and after 15 m notice an intriguing tunnel through which boats were hauled. This gives access to a secret cove: if you wish to explore it, take care because it is extremely slippery underfoot.

Daymarks used in navigation

- Continue up a signed narrow shady lane for 100 m, then turn right. Continue uphill quite steeply for 300 m, with the help of granite blocks.

Gwennap Head lookout

Sea cliffs beyond Land's End

- Cross a boulder wall, then find a stone wall on your left which you follow for 50 m. The path then continues slightly leftwards to St Levan, but you fork right (slightly south of east) at a low SWCP sign.
- For 300 m the path slopes gently downhill, then more steeply with steps, to cross a stream and pass St Levan's Well above the sands of Porth Chapel beach.

St Levan's Well

- Follow the path as it rises gently for 300 m, eventually with steps. A further 300 m on the level brings you to the car park of Minack Theatre. Cross the car park and, to explore the theatre, use the entrance on your right to enter and exit: see panel.
- Back on the SWCP, continue past the theatre on your left towards the coast. Eventually you descend lots of very steep and irregular granite steps: take care.

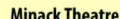
Minack Theatre
The Minack Theatre is a famous open-air performance venue. Perched on granite cliffs and set in lush gardens, it overlooks the spectacular panorama of Porthcurno Bay. It was hand-built over the winter of 1931 and into 1932 by Rowena Cade, the owner of Minack House, and her gardener. The summer theatre season runs from May to September. The theatre has an exhibition and café and is open for visits year-round, but not at performance times: see www.minack.com.

- From the bottom of the steps, continue for 150 m towards Porthcurno Beach, keeping left if you want to avoid the beach itself. Cross the track at the head of the cove which could take you on an inland detour to the Cable Station Inn 370 m away. Porthcurno Telegraph Museum offers insight into the earliest use of submarine cables (open daily in season, otherwise part-time: www.telegraphmuseum.org).
- Continue on the path as it climbs quite steeply to the next headland. Once on top, head north and after 100 m arrive at a junction with another path that crosses east-west.
- Turn 90° right, and after a further 150 m keep left, avoiding the path that branches downwards to your right.

  If travelling in the reverse direction, stay very alert here.

Minack Theatre

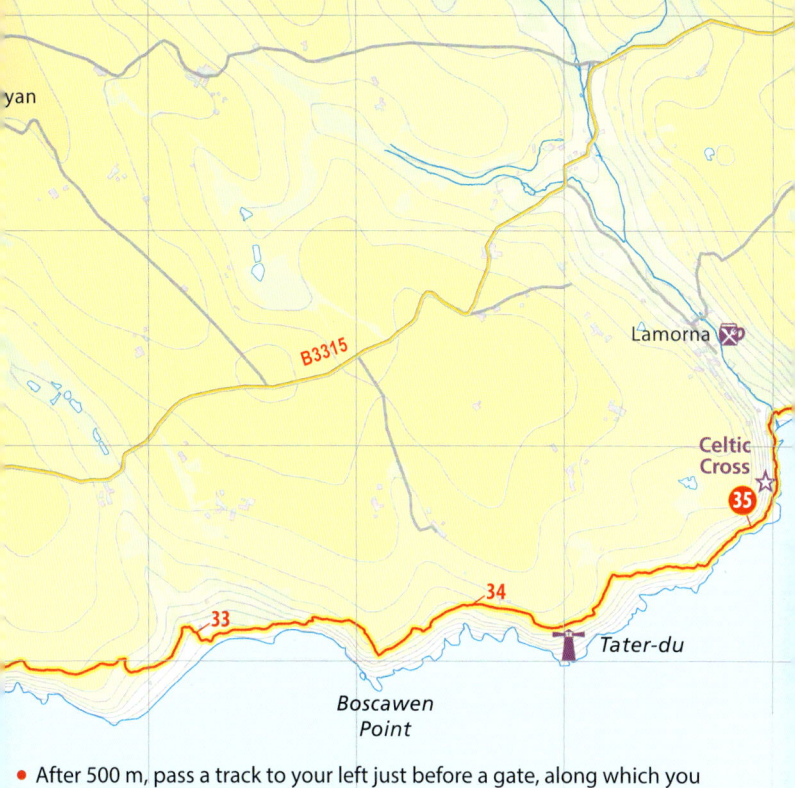

- After 500 m, pass a track to your left just before a gate, along which you can reach Treen, 500 m inland. After a further 600 m of SWCP you could take the path to the right to investigate the remains of Treryn Dinas, an Iron Age fort.
- The path now curves north and reaches Penberth Cove after a further 1 km.
- Go around the cove, passing toilets on your left, then head uphill again. About 100 m after levelling out on the headland, follow signs carefully: the path makes a 90° right turn, so don't be tempted to go straight on instead.

If travelling in the reverse direction, stay particularly alert here.

Approaching Treen Cliff

Penberth Cove

- After 150 m stay left, avoiding the path that branches downwards to your right.
- Continue for 2 km, with the flora becoming more varied as you pass alongside hedgerows, across a grass swathe mown through scrub, eventually reaching woodland.
- For the first time on this walk you walk through woodland – part of the Boscawen SSSI (Site of Special Scientific Interest). After 100 m pass a house on your right and immediately go through two gates marked with the white acorn sign: ignore a stile to the left.
- Descend steps then cross a track and then a small brook. After a further 50 m, the path takes to the bouldery beach for 50 m. Pass a vast rusting overturned tripod, turn left and head uphill, at first on granite steps.

Along the bouldery beach

Ford at Penberth Cove

- Follow the path for 2 km, under a low tree canopy at first, then twisting through ferns, with a final pull uphill to reach Tater-du.
- Its lighthouse, Cornwall's most recent, nestles behind locked gates, inside Tater-du SSSI. It was built after the loss of a Spanish coaster and 11 crew in 1963, and it's best viewed just before a gate further along the path.
- Now follow the path as its swings north-east and descend steps after 500 m. After a further 200 m, a picturesque Celtic cross stands on your right, and the path turns north to Lamorna Cove, with café, toilets and car park.
- Curve around to the head of the cove. Here the road to your left leads to the Lamorna Wink, a pub 500 m inland, where you can await a pick-up if pre-arranged with the hosts of your overnight accommodation. The Wink took its name from the locally recognised code sign that smuggled goods were available.
- For a good view of St Michael's Mount, still 9 km distant, follow directions of the first bullet on page 54, afterwards retracing your steps. This detour adds about 1·5 km return.

Tater-du Lighthouse

Lamorna Wink pub

View back to Lamorna

3·5 Lamorna to Penzance

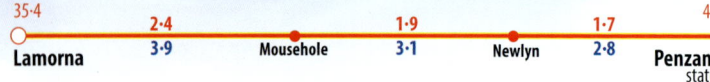

Distance	6·1 miles 9·8 km
Terrain	generally good going underfoot, eventually becoming pavement en route to Penzance
Grade	mainly gentle gradients; altitude gain and loss 225 m
Food and drink	many options at Mousehole and Newlyn
Summary	a short finale that starts with a nature reserve, then returns to the bustling world of tourism and commercial fishing

35·4 Lamorna — 2·4 / 3·9 — Mousehole — 1·9 / 3·1 — Newlyn — 1·7 / 2·8 — 41·5 Penzance station

- From Lamorna Cove, cross over a concrete bridge, passing toilets on your left, and keeping right to pass between two houses. Continue on fairly flat heath until you reach a brief descent via steps to Carn-du, where St Michael's Mount becomes visible.

- Follow the path north-east for the next 2 km through Kemyel Crease – a Cornwall Wildlife Trust Nature Reserve of mixed pine and oak woodland.

- Emerge onto a track, then a road, passing lovely houses on your right, with commanding views over the sea at Point Spaniard. You are at the outskirts of Mousehole. SWCP signs here are sparse, so stay alert to stick to the official route.

- Follow the road and bear right to reach a car park. Cross it to reach the harbour – its tiny protective seaward entry 'as small as a mousehole'. Skirt around the harbour, where the SWCP makes a brief excursion inland on narrow streets, to reach another car park.

- Exit through the far end of a parking area and keep left to emerge onto pavement beside The Parade. Turn right to follow this road, whose name soon changes to Cliff Road, after 500 m passing the memorial to Penlee Lifeboat on your right.

Approaching Mousehole

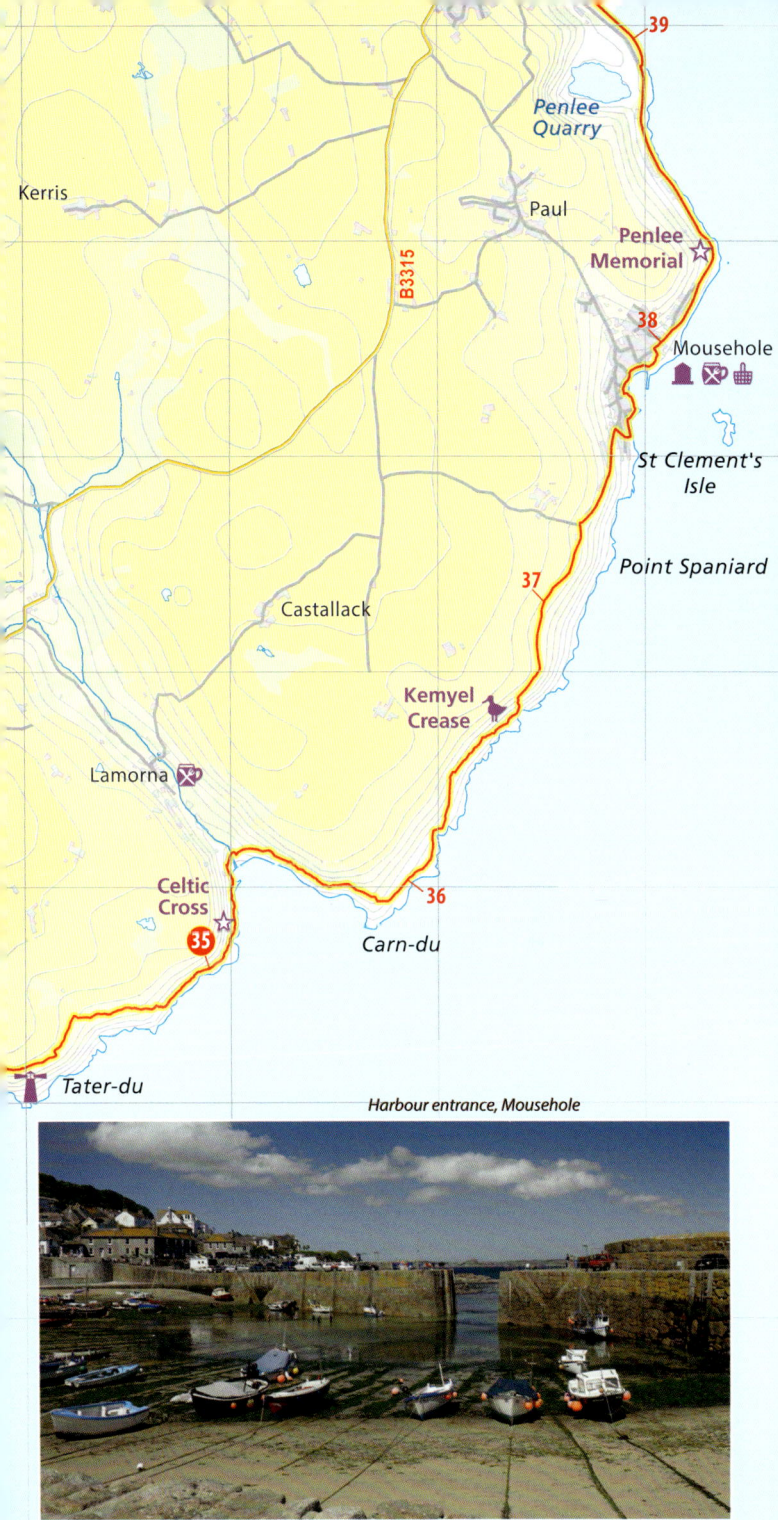

Harbour entrance, Mousehole

55

- Cliff Road continues beyond Penlee Point, passing two SSSIs. Just after Penlee Quarry bear right onto a cycle track that runs between the road and the shore for nearly 600 m.
- After the cycle track rejoin the road (now called Fore Street), soon reaching the South Pier at Newlyn with its tidal observatory.
- Follow the medieval quayside along Lower Green Street. After 500 m bear right as signed for Newlyn Art Gallery and pass the Fisherman's statue soon after the gallery. You are now only 2·5 km short of Penzance railway station.
- Continue on the pavement beside the road, with the conurbation on the outskirts of Penzance on your left.
- As you walk along the coast on Penzance's Western Promenade Road, the tower of St Mary's parish church becomes ever more prominent.

Fisherman's statue, Newlyn

 Newlyn
Newlyn became the principal place at which the Ordnance Survey determined Mean Sea Level between 1915 and 1921 because the tide came in from the Atlantic unimpeded, the granite geology was stable, and because it was close to the Continental Shelf. It was a centre of Cornwall's vital pilchard industry, and its 40 acres of harbour are still home to one of the UK's largest fishing fleets. From the 1880s onwards it was also home to the Newlyn School of painting.

- The road becomes Battery Road and bends left just after Jubilee Pool Café to become The Quay. Take care: some stretches lack any pavement.
- At the end of the harbour, look very carefully for a tiny acorn waymark attached to the blank rear of a huge traffic sign. Here bear right to enter the Long Stay car park. After a further 200 m you reach the coast where you will find the Tourist Information Centre, rail and bus stations, toilets and a café.
- Congratulations: you have completed this guidebook's section of the SWCP and may now be heading to your accommodation or going home. However, if you want to continue the SWCP to Marazion, see page 59.

St Mary's parish church, Penzance

Penzance harbour, with St Mary's tower

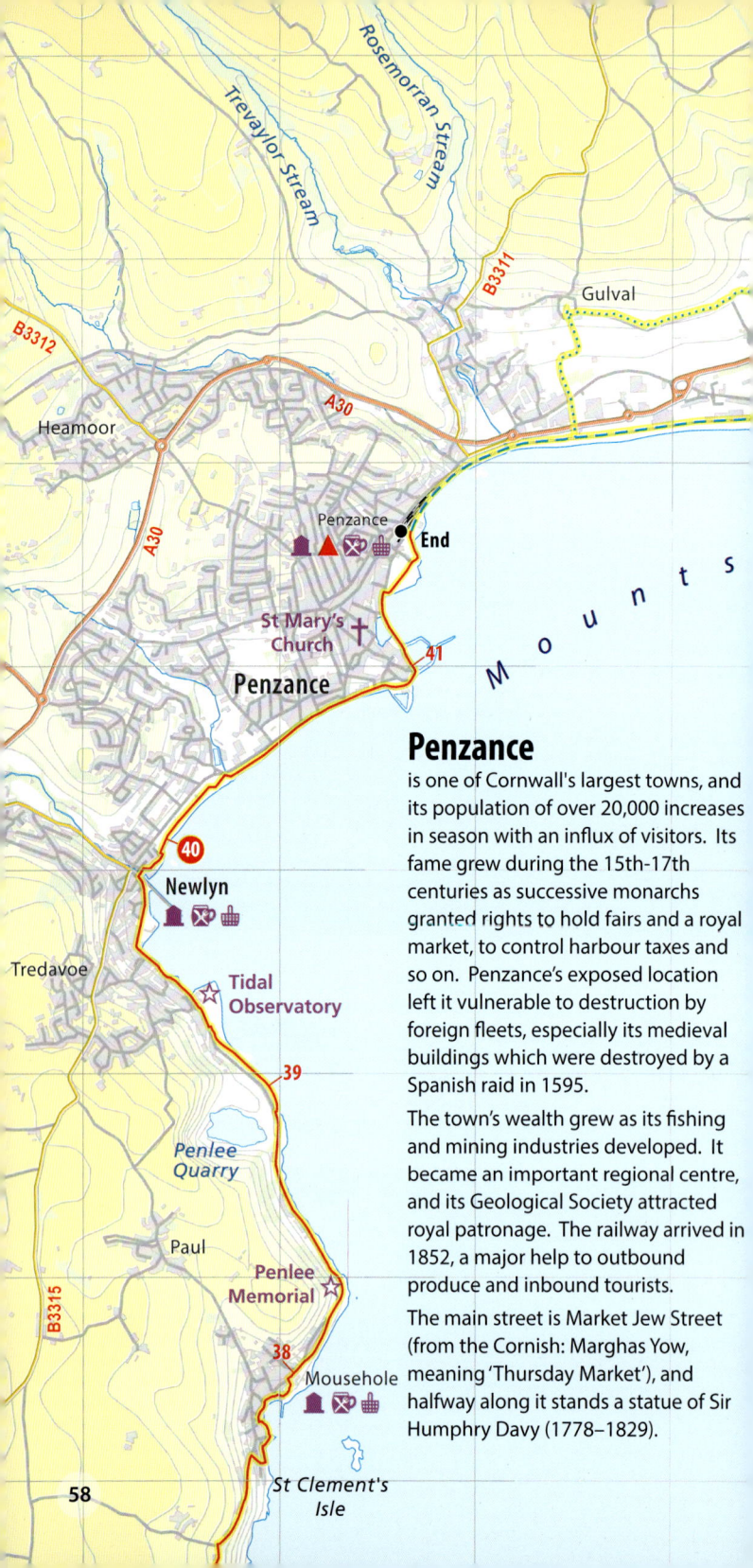

Penzance

is one of Cornwall's largest towns, and its population of over 20,000 increases in season with an influx of visitors. Its fame grew during the 15th-17th centuries as successive monarchs granted rights to hold fairs and a royal market, to control harbour taxes and so on. Penzance's exposed location left it vulnerable to destruction by foreign fleets, especially its medieval buildings which were destroyed by a Spanish raid in 1595.

The town's wealth grew as its fishing and mining industries developed. It became an important regional centre, and its Geological Society attracted royal patronage. The railway arrived in 1852, a major help to outbound produce and inbound tourists.

The main street is Market Jew Street (from the Cornish: Marghas Yow, meaning 'Thursday Market'), and halfway along it stands a statue of Sir Humphry Davy (1778–1829).

Davy was the son of a local craftsman who was apprenticed to a surgeon. Later he pioneered electrolysis to isolate chemical elements, and in 1815, prompted by Newcastle miners, he invented the Davy lamp to avoid methane explosions.

Chapel Street, off Market Jew Street, houses some of the town's finest buildings, including the showy Egyptian House, built in the 1830s and now an apartment block. Nelson's victory at Trafalgar and his death were first announced at the nearby Union Hotel. Further west is Morrab Street with Penlee House Gallery and Museum, which covers local history, archaeology and the world-famous paintings of the Newlyn School artists: *www.penleehouse.org.uk*.

Beyond Penzance

From Penzance, some readers will return home, but most will want to visit St Michael's Mount: see pages 68-9. Access to the island is by tidal causeway, and opening hours are limited, so plan your visit: see panel on page 69. Reach Marazion slipway on foot or by bus: either walk 2·9 miles (4·6 km) along the SWCP on a cycle track starting from the north-east corner of the car park beside Penzance station, or take a bus along the coast – about 10 minutes – then take the causeway or boat: details on *www.stmichaelsmount.co.uk*.

Afterwards you can walk back to St Ives as described on pages 70-77. (You could instead bypass St Michael's Mount and take the version of St Michael's Way via Gulval shown as a dotted line on the map above, described on *www.britishpilgrimage.org*. We do not recommend this complicated route which involves more road-walking.)

St Michael's Mount

St Michael's Mount was built by the giants Cormoran and his wife Cormelian. Giants abound in Cornish legend and explain the presence of selected headlands and large rocks such as the granite tors atop Trencrom Hill.

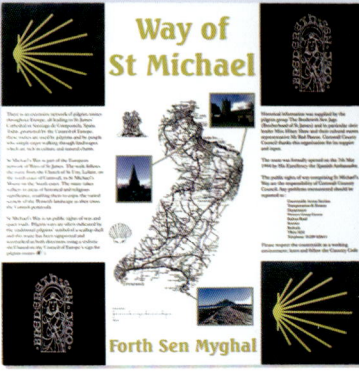

Stone Age finds suggest early human presence, and the mount may be the island of Ictis - described as a tin trading centre by the pre-Christian historian Diodorus Siculus. Later, Edward the Confessor gave the site to the Benedictine order of Mont Saint-Michel, after local sightings of St Michael, the patron saint of mariners. It housed a monastery from the 8th to the early 11th centuries, during the medieval rise of monasticism and pilgrimage and the arrival of missionary-monks from Ireland and Wales.

The monks were followed by pilgrims, some of whom continued to Santiago de Compostela in Spain, and who established nearby St Michael's Way as a path to avoid sailing the wrecking waters off Land's End. It developed as a busy port with a population that reached 300.

The mount saw conflict during the Wars of the Roses, and the 12th century church and priory were extended to become a fully-fledged castle. It later returned to quiet religious life until the effects of Henry VIII's dissolution of the monasteries reached the area in 1548.

Across the causeway to St Michael's Mount and castle

St Michael's Mount from the south

The mount was eventually sold to the St Aubyn family in 1659. The site was re-fortified in 1940 as part of the south coast defences against possible German invasion, and was gifted to the National Trust in 1954.

The mount offers sights of a Bronze Age hoard, gun batteries, other weapons, and suits of armour from the Wars of the Roses and the Civil War. The Mount also has a sub-tropical garden with exotic flowers and trees planted in terraces that descend to the sea. The granite rock acts as a heat sink that moderates the location's exposure and frost.

Plan your visit

The Mount is accessible from Marazion. At low tide you can walk the 500 metre cobbled causeway, or at high tide you can instead take a 5-minute boat ride.

Visit **www.stmichaelsmount.co.uk** to check opening times: although the causeway is a public right of way, all of the island's facilities are closed on Saturdays and there is little to see. To plan your visit, consult that website and also that of the National Trust; entrance is free to NT members, see page 71.

4 St Ives via St Michael's Way

Distance	**8·5 miles 13·6 km**
Terrain	easy paths through fields; occasional minor roads, in places without pavements
Grade	some undulation, but gentle gradients apart from Knill's Monument; height gain / loss 380m
Food and drink	Marazion, Ludgvan, St Ives; farms on route; Carbis Bay
Summary	a pleasant stroll through classic Cornish countryside; needs careful navigation because waymarking is sparse in places

```
0·0      1·6         2·7              2·5          1·6           8·5
●————————●———————————●————————P———————●————————————●—————————————○
Marazion  2·6 Ludgvan  4·4   Trencrom Hill  4·1  Knill's    2·6  St Ives
slipway                                          Monument        station
```

We recommend you to take a GPS-enabled device (e.g. smartphone: see page 71): the offroad parts of this route are sparsely waymarked.

- From Marazion slipway car park, return along the esplanade towards Penzance. Make a right-left dogleg to cross Folleyfield car park, then cross a footbridge over the Red River, just south of the road bridge.

- Continue next to the road on sand until you reach a 40 mph sign. Here cross the road and pass through an obvious gap in the hedge. Cross an overflow car park, exiting on the opposite side. Turn right and after just 20 m reach the fingerpost on your left for St Michael's Way.

Fingerpost pointing north across Marazion Marsh

- Continue on grass, angling right over the Red River by a footbridge. After 400 m cross a rail track carefully via a level crossing.

- About 300 m after the railway, reach a stile at the A394 and cross the road. Go over another stile to enter a field, and follow its edge. Ludgvan church becomes visible ahead.

- Exit the field over a stile. Cross the A30 road heading right, but immediately bear left as signed to Ludgvan Leaze. After 200 m (opposite a large Accident Repair shed) turn left at the fingerpost (mile 1·4).

St Michael's Mount from the north

- Over the next 600 m follow fingerposts to cross a field by its edge, cross a lane, cross another field-edge, and after crossing a cattle grid of granite, turn left at the B3309 (Church Hill) and continue to the White Hart pub and then Ludgvan church.
- Turn right past the church tower to head north on a lane at a fingerpost.

Ludgvan church

- Continue mainly north for 350 m downhill to a stream, and cross it. Enter a field, cross it and exit over a stile. Continue uphill to reach and bypass a seven-bar metal gate. Continue straight on to reach a tarmac lane.

Unmarked gap in the hedgerow at mile 2·3

- At the fingerpost, turn left along the lane for 140 m. Just before a rusty gate, turn right through the unmarked gap in a hedgerow (**mile 2·3**).
- Keeping a tall pylon on your left, cross the field-edge, at first towards solar panels on the hillside ahead.
- Angle diagonally left (north-west) across the next field, and exit by an unmarked gate. Cross the next field, exiting via a wide unmarked gap in the stone wall: ignore the metal gate next to it.
- In this next field, bear slightly left while heading downhill towards a metal gate. Just 10 m further on, cross a stile, finally with a reassuring waymarker. After a further 50 m through the wood, cross a stream and go over the stile immediately after.
- Bear left to climb the hill and reach a gateway at the field's north corner. Cross the waymarked stile into the next field, still climbing.
- Exit the field across a waymarked stile and continue straight ahead on the tarmac lane to pass Boskennal Farm on your left (**mile 2·7**).
- About 350 m after the farm, turn sharp right at a low sign on the right. Continue on the tarmac to cross the Red River by granite ford or footbridge.

Crossing the Red River (by ford or footbridge)

- After 15 m turn left to enter a field via a gate. Cross the field and soon fork left to cross a stile marked 'Public Footpath' (**mile 3·1**).
- Continue uphill then cross a waymarked stile. Cross a further field keeping a large wind turbine to your left, and exit via a waymarked gate to reach a bridleway (**mile 3·6**).
- Cross the bridleway then cross two further fields via wooden kissing-gates with waymarks, keeping Trembethow Farm on your left.

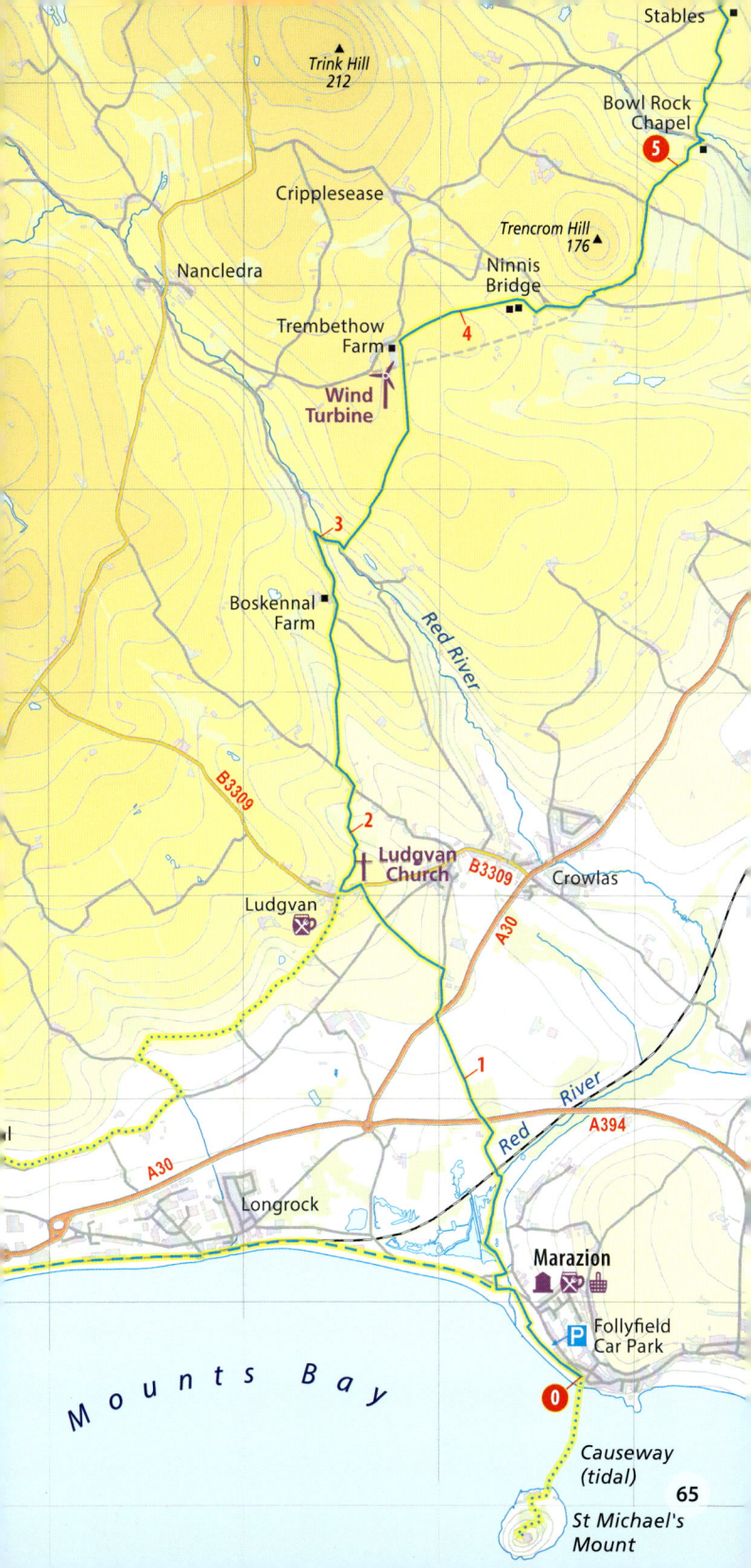

View backwards before Trencrom Lane dogleg

- Over the next 700 m, cross two fields via wooden gates, then angle north-eastwards to reach a meandering path. After 50 m reach and cross a stile at a large wooden hut (**mile 4·1**).
- Continue for 100 m to reach a stream but do not cross it. Keeping the stream on your left, after 100 m reach two cottages at Ninnis Bridge, the first one named 'Methodist Chapel'.
- Immediately after the second cottage, turn left along a tarmac lane. About 60 m later fork right, soon merging leftwards onto a wider lane.
- After 150 m, at a car park, a fingerpost points to the left for an optional ascent of Trencrom Hill, a prehistoric site.
- Follow fingerposts to skirt the right-hand side of the hill – unless keen to detour to its summit at 175 m. For the last 180 m keep to the right-most fork.
- After a total of 580 m from the Trencrom Hill car park, reach and cross a stone stile at a tarmac lane. Cross the lane to enter the left-most of the two fields facing you, using unmarked stone steps. Descend to the far right-hand corner of the field, and cross a waymarked stile.
- Continue for 50 m to reach a house named 'Bowl Rock Chapel' at a tarmac road. Cross the road and turn left for just 20 m, where you turn right (mile 5·2). Pass several houses including Bowl Rock Cottage on a driveable track.
- From Bowl Rock Cottage, continue generally northwards for 550 m: at first go uphill to reach and cross a waymarked stone stile, eventually to find Standing Stone Stables on your right. Cross a stone stile through the hedge on your left. Follow the edge of the field parallel to the stables' driveway, and exit over a dilapidated stile.

View north from Knill's Monument

National Coastwatch Lookout

- Make a right-left dogleg across Trencrom Lane (mile 5·6). Follow the waymarked post to pass large dilapidated sheds and enter the second field on your right (not signed).
- Cross the field diagonally and exit near the opposite corner via a stone stile. Cross a very narrow track. Continue north for 170 m to a tarmac road (Laity Lane) at mile 5·9.
- Turn left along Laity Lane, which after 150 m swings right, later bending left, and follow it north-west for a total of 1·3 km.
- Leave the road at its 90° left bend (mile 6·9) and turn right towards Knill's Monument: there is no waymarker, but the obelisk is visible 300 m away to the south-east
- Leave the monument on an unmarked northbound path. After 130 m, turn right at a fingerpost down Steeple Lane. Follow this tarmac road as it descends past houses.

> **Knill's Monument**
> This obelisk stands 55 ft/17 m tall and overlooks St Ives Bay. It was built in 1782 as a mausoleum, by John Knill (1733–1811), the Collector of Customs at St Ives (1762-82) and its mayor (1767). His will specified a bizarre ceremony to be carried out at the obelisk every five years. It involves ten young dancing girls from the families of fishermen dressed in white, two widows in black, and a fiddler to play the 'Furry Dance'. This drama is still enacted on a five-year cycle.

Knill's Monument

- After 700 m reach a T-junction (unmarked) and turn right onto Higher Tregenna Road, then immediately turn right again onto St Ives Road.
- After 150 m turn left down a track (Wheal Margery) at an indistinct waymark. Stay on the downhill track for 100 m to pass a road on your left and continue to a kissing-gate.
- Pass through the gate and for 100 m continue on the path as it bears left and reaches a T-junction with the SWCP.
- The fingerpost points right towards Lelant (and Carbis Bay station), but for St Ives instead turn left along Hain Walk for 600 m. At an obvious bend in the Walk continue straight ahead at a low fingerpost and join a path towards St Ives.
- After 150 m cross the railway by a footbridge, follow the zigzags downhill and turn left beside the coast. Within 300 m of the railway, you reach St Ives station.

St Michael's Way meets the SWCP

Alternative ending at Lelant

Instead of St Ives, you may prefer to finish at Lelant, 4 km south-east of St Ives, through which most pilgrims passed. To avoid the dangerous waters around Land's End, those heading to Santiago de Compostela used to land at Lelant, pray at St Uny's church for safe travel, and continue on foot along St Michael's Way to Marazion to embark for France and Spain.

If so, turn right at the fingerpost at mile 7·8 and follow the waymarked SWCP above Carbis Bay. Then drop down to cross the railway and traverse Carbis Bay Resort. Continue uphill and turn left at a fingerpost. Descend steps and stay on the SWCP for 2 km above Porth Kidney Sands. Turn right to cross beneath the railway. Sunken paths guide you through the golf course to St Uny's church at Lelant. From the church, you can continue on the waymarked SWCP to Lelant rail station and return to St Ives, or go home.

West over Carbis Bay

5 Reference

Development of the trail

The South West Coast Path has a long history. Some of its sections were likely trodden by our forebears from the Stone, Bronze and Iron Ages. As smuggling grew in the remote county of Cornwall, the authorities set up a coast watch to suppress it, and the coast guards developed cliff-top paths to scan the seas and peer down on remote coves. The path was used for this purpose until the early 20th century, and thereafter to support coastal defences during two World Wars.

The South West Coast Path evolved into a walking trail that opened in stages during the 1970s. The first section to open in 1973 was in Cornwall, culminating in 1978 with the Somerset & North Devon stage and designation as a National Trail. The SWCP Association is a major charity founded in 1973. It campaigned successfully for this trail from 1973, and still works hard to sustain and improve it:
   www.southwestcoastpath.org.uk.
Check for route updates on their page:
   bit.ly/SWCP-route

St Michael's Way, the optional link route that completes our circuit, developed in medieval times as pilgrims to Santiago de Compostela travelled overland to Marazion to avoid the waters around Land's End, as did some traders. The route was re-established in 1994, and since 2015 has been overseen by the Friends of St Michael's Way:
   www.stmichaelsway.net.

Visitor information & accommodation

Two websites provide valuable sources on accommodation, events, and the towns and villages; the first also provides daily weather and tide times:
The Cornwall Guide
   www.cornwalls.co.uk
Visit Cornwall
   www.visitcornwall.com/places/west-cornwall

Route links

Our website offers many links to towns, villages, museums, mines and sources of accommodation including where to find campsites along the route. Visit
   www.rucsacs.com/books/lec and scroll down to reach *Route links*.

Support services

Our website offers links to companies offering holiday planning and baggage transfer. Visit
   www.rucsacs.com/books/lec and scroll down to reach *Support services*.

Examples include:
Contours Holidays specialises in inclusive self-guided walking holidays with a choice of itineraries:
   www.contours.co.uk

Encounter Walking also arranges self-guided walking holidays and pride themselves in meeting unusual requests:
   www.encounterwalkingholidays.com

Celtic Trails arrange self-guided walks on selected segments of the SWCP including St Ives to Penzance:
   www.celtictrailswalkingholidays.co.uk

Further reading

Armitage, Simon *Walking away: further travels with a troubadour on the South West Coast Path* Faber & Faber 2016. The poet and raconteur describes his walk busking along the northern segment of the SWCP, including the stretch from St Ives to Land's End.

Camm, Simon *The geology and landscape of Cornwall and the Isles of Scilly*:
Alison Hodge, 2011. An accessible, expert and well-illustrated introduction to the geology of the area.

Gogerty, Clare *Tin Coast*, Cornwall, National Trust, 2017. 32-page booklet about the mining landmarks between Pendeen Watch and Cape Cornwall.

Graham, Winston *Ross Poldark* Pan Books, 1997 The first novel of the 12-volume series twice serialised by BBC, vividly dramatising life in the area in the 19th century

Van der Kiste, John *The Little Book of Cornwall* The History Press, 2013
Quirky guide to Cornwall's men and women, towns and countryside, history, natural history, literary and artistic achievements, agriculture, transport and industry

Winn, Raynor *The Salt Path* Penguin Books, 2019 Uplifting memoir of a couple who walked the SWCP after becoming homeless shortlisted for various literary awards.

Maps (printed and online)

Ordnance Survey, Explorer 102 Land's End (updated in 2019) covers the whole Penwith peninsula and beyond at 1:25,000. In 2020 it cost £8.99 (or £14.99 for weatherproof).

Our online route map shows the route in great detail and can be zoomed repeatedly: visit
   www.rucsacs.com/books/lec and click on the map graphic.

Global Positioning System (GPS)

GPS is a satellite-based navigation system which is free to use. It relies on a network of satellites orbiting the earth at high altitude. By comparing information on satellite distances, GPS can calculate your location very accurately. It does not require a phone signal, but it needs a clear sight of the sky. Anyone with a smart phone can download a GPS app (free or very cheap) and learn how to use it. GPS can be a very useful addition to map and compass navigation – for a quick check at a junction, in mist or cloud, and to pinpoint your location in case of an emergency. Download our GPS route file from
   www.rucsacs.com/books/lec – scroll down to reach *Bonus content*.

Transport and travel

For journeys from anywhere to anywhere:
   www.rome2rio.com
For UK train travel:
   www.nationalrail.co.uk and
   www.thetrainline.com
Buses along the Land's End peninsula (run by First Kernow):
   www.firstgroup.com/cornwall/plan-journey/timetables

Weather, wind and tides

For weather forecasts by region, visit
   www.metoffice.gov.uk or
   www.bbc.co.uk/weather
We thank Iowa State University
   mesonet.agron.iastate.edu for wind rose data which appears in simplified form on page 7.

View tide times up to 7 days ahead at St Ives, Cape Cornwall, Sennen Cove and Penzance (Newlyn), or 90 days ahead if you subscribe:
   www.tidetimes.org.uk

Cornish Language Office

Cornwall Council maintains a Cornish Language Office and encourages its staff to use words and phrases in Cornish:
   www.cornwall.gov.uk.

National Trust

Source of information on the heritage coastline, mining and St Michael's Mount. Admission is free to members:
   www.nationaltrust.org.uk/search?query=cornwall

Notes for novices

For those new to long-distance walking, the Rucksack Readers website
   www.rucsacs.com
offers advice: scroll to the foot of the home page for the link.

Acknowledgements

We thank the South West Coast Path Association and British Pilgrimage Trust who provided the GPX files upon which, after editing, our mapping and GPX files are based. We thank also Lindsay Merriman for painstaking proofreading.

Photo credits

Glen Batten 29 (lower); Berkshire Bus Pics 12; Ian Clydesdale 52 (middle), 53 (middle), back cover; Lynne Kirton 25 (all butterflies); Max Landsberg 10 (all six), 11 (all three), 14, 30, 31, 32, 32-33, 33, 34, 35, 36 (both), 37, 38 (both), 39, 40, 40-41, 42 (both), 43, 44 (both), 44-45, 45, 46-7, 47-48, 48, 50, 51, 52 (upper & lower), 53 (upper & lower), 54, 55, 56, 60, 60-61, 62, 62-63, 63, 64 (both), 66 (both), 67, 69 (both); Jacquetta Megarry 27 (upper); Malcolm Osman 18, 20 (upper), 20/21, 22 (both), 27 (lower), 28 (lower), 68; CharliePhillipsimages.co.uk 34 (lower); Gordon Simm 25 (upper), 26 (middle); *www.cornwalls.co.uk* 49.

We thank also *Dreamstime.com* with the following photographers: Phillip Gray front cover; Chris Dorney title page; paop 4-5; Mick Blakey 6-7; Steve Roberts 16-17; Brian Kushner 23 (upper); Andreanita 24 (upper); Mikelane45 24 (middle); Robert Adam Charlesworth 24 (lower); Davemhuntphotography 26 (upper); Lukas Blazek 26 (lower); Bonandbon Dw 61 (upper); and *Shutterstock.com* with RMC42 9; Boris Stroujko 28 (upper); aaabbbccc 29 (upper); Ian Woolcock 56-7; Andy333 57 (upper); and *Wikimedia Commons* with Jim Champion 18 (middle) and 19 (upper); and with Anagoria 21 (upper).

Index

A
accommodation 8
B
birdlife 24
Botallack 22, 40
Bronze Age 19 61
buses 12
butterflies 25
C
Cape Cornwall 42
Carbis Bay 28, 69
Celts 19
chough 24
Cornish language 15
Countryside Code 13
Crowns Mine 22, 39
D
Davy, Sir Humphry 58
development of the trail 70
direction 5
dogs 13
dolphin, bottlenose 23
duration 8
F
facilities 8
fox 26
G
gannet 24
Geevor Mine 18, 22, 38
geology 16-18
GPS, advice and file 11, 62, 71
gradients and profile 10-11
H
habitats 23
Hepworth, Barbara 20, 28
history (of Cornwall) 19-20
I
Ice Age 17
Iron Age 36, 51
K
Knill's Monument 68
L
Lamorna 53
land animals 26
Land's End 5, 6, 7, 16-17, 18, 25, 44-5, 46
Lawrence, D H 20, 34
Lelant 69
Levant Mine 18, 22, 38
Lizard, the 16, 18, 24
Logan Rock 18
Ludgvan church 62, 63
M
Maen Castle 45

maps 71
Marazion 57, 59, 61, 62
Middle Ages 19
Minack Theatre 50
mining 20, 21-22
Mousehole 54
N
Newlyn 56
Notes for novices 71
O
otter 26
oystercatcher 25
P
packing checklist 14
Pendeen Watch (lighthouse) 33, 37
Penlee 54, 56
Penwith 5, 16, 71
Penzance 58
peregrine falcon 23, 24
pilgrims 11
Poldark 22
preparation 5
pronunciation 15
Q
quoit 19
R
Roman occupation 19
route links 70
S
safety 13
seals, grey and common 26
smuggling 19
South West Coast Path 4, 70
St Ives 28, 29. 30, 59
St Michael's Way 11
stages 8
stonechat 24
support services 70
SWCP Association 70
T
Tate St Ives 20, 28, 30
terrain 10
thrift 27
tides 71
transport and travel 12, 71
W
waymarking 11
weather 7
weather 13, 71
wildlife 23-27
wind 7, 13, 71
Z
Zennor 19, 34, 35